QUILT
TALK

12 Chatty Projects

Paper-Pieced Alphabet with Symbols & Numbers

Sam Hunter

stashBOOKS®

an imprint of C&T Publishing

Text copyright © 2014 by Sam Hunter

Photography and Artwork copyright © 2014 by C&T Publishing, Inc.

PUBLISHER: Amy Marson

CREATIVE DIRECTOR: Gailen Runge

ART DIRECTOR/COVER DESIGNER: Kristy Zacharias

EDITORS: S. Michele Fry, Liz Aneloski, and Karla Menaugh

TECHNICAL EDITORS: Ellen Pahl and Debbie Rodgers

BOOK DESIGNER: Christina Jarumay Fox

PRODUCTION COORDINATOR: Jenny Davis

PRODUCTION EDITOR: Alice Mace Nakanishi

ILLUSTRATORS: Tim Manibusan and Sam Hunter

PHOTO ASSISTANT: Mary Peyton Peppo

Style photography by Nissa Brehmer and instructional photography by Diane Pedersen, unless otherwise noted

Published by Stash Books, an imprint of C&T Publishing, Inc., P.O. Box 1456, Lafayette, CA 94549

Library of Congress Cataloging-in-Publication Data

Hunter, Sam, 1961-

  Quilt talk : paper-pieced alphabet with symbols & numbers : 12 chatty projects / Sam Hunter.

     pages cm

  ISBN 978-1-60705-888-5 (soft cover)

1. Quilting--Patterns. 2. Patchwork--Patterns. 3. Patchwork quilts. 4. Lettering in art. 5. Words in art. 6. Alphabet in art. I. Title.

  TT835.H8537 2014

  746.46--dc23

                            2014003189

Printed in China

10 9 8 7 6 5 4 3 2 1

DEDICATION

*For the one and only Stevo
—I love you (you know).*

ACKNOWLEDGMENTS

To be involved in the arts is to be surrounded by brilliant, generous, and talented friends— in my case a wildly eclectic and loving tribe, without whom life would be a far less colorful adventure. I hesitate to name names, knowing that I will undoubtedly miss someone special (and I doubt that you want to read the book equivalent of the dreadfully boring acceptance speech that endlessly lists people you'll never meet). Suffice it to say that no creative project is made in a vacuum, and the village that surrounds this one is mighty, powerful, and humbling. You know who you are, I thank you, and you rock!

TABLE OF

PROJECTS

INTRODUCTION

> "What is the use
> of a book," thought Alice,
> "without pictures
> or conversations?"
> —LEWIS CARROLL

I'm a word girl. I love words and wordplay. I love that our language constantly changes and evolves to meet our needs, and that we have thousands of words at our disposal to shape what we say. I find it endlessly fascinating that despite all these words we can still struggle to find the right ones. Or, conversely, we can say something perfectly in the briefest phrase. I love conversation almost as much as I love chocolate!

I spent my formative years in England, well saturated in Shakespeare and Dickens, but also in Benny Hill and Monty Python. I grew up steeped in the fine arts of wordplay and subtle humor that seem to be an everyday part of British DNA. I should warn you, though, that I don't sound very English at all in person, unless I've been on the phone to family (or am knotted up with nerves). Then it all comes out … you might take the girl out of England, but you can't take the England out of this girl!

As a teenager, and before the dawn of the personal computer, I spent a lot of time playing with lettering catalogs. I was (and am still) captivated by the way letters are formed and how they can be used, and I have often wished I had known back then that designing fonts was an actual career that I could have pursued.

As a teen, I was fortunate to be able to spend time with my grandmothers. Nanny Hunter knitted and crocheted; Nanny Janes knitted, tatted lace, and owned a Singer treadle sewing machine. Although my mom bravely let me use her electric machine (to make Barbie clothes) when I was seven, it was time on the treadle that really lit me up about sewing. I found quilting in my twenties, and the rest, as they say, is history.

As I watched the world of quilting expand into ever new territories, I found myself thinking that playing with text was a possible next frontier. I liked the idea that, through the use of text, a quilt could really start a conversation. And personally, of course, I was eager to play with words and fabric at the same time. So I gave myself the challenge of designing an alphabet that was both usable and readable, and at the same time easily mastered with modest sewing skills.

This book is a marriage of my love of fiber and my love of words. In creating the characters of this alphabet, my font-designing aspirations have been realized in a way that I never could have imagined all those years ago. You are holding the result in your hands, and I hope you have as much fun playing with this alphabet as I do.

P.S. When you have completed your *Quilt Talk* project, be sure to post it on Instagram using #quilttalk.

Photo by Larry Lytle

BASICS

Rather than take up valuable pages with a chapter on the basics of quilting, I have opted to give you more project options. Thus, this book assumes you have mastered the following basic quilting skills:

- Using a rotary cutter, cutting mat, and rulers
- Setting up your sewing machine to sew with a decent (not necessarily perfect but mostly consistent) ¼″ seam
- Layering and basting a quilt for quilting
- Hand or machine quilting (or you can hire someone to do it for you!)
- Adding and finishing binding

If you need to brush up on any of these skills, pop by your local quilt store for some help, consult some basic quilting books, or load up some Internet video tutorials. For some book and DVD ideas, see Resources (page 142).

Additional Techniques

In the Appendix (page 134), you will find some brief descriptions of techniques that are needed in some projects:

- How to join strips with a diagonal seam (both for strip units within quilts and for bindings)
- How to piece a "snowball" corner
- How to make and add a sleeve to the back of a quilt

A Few Words on the Projects

- Paper piecing is easy! Yes, you really can master it— it's all just straight lines! With no curved seams or complicated construction, every project in the book is designed to be quite easy once you get the hang of paper piecing.
- Sometimes the order in which you cut doesn't match the order in which you sew. If keeping the parts straight gets complicated, use sticky notes or painter's tape to mark your pieces.
- Don't limit yourself to the projects in the book. Several people have shared ideas for their next projects (page 51). Use the projects and those additional ideas as a launching point for your own designs.

A Few Words on Quilt Backs

- I have listed the sizes for backing as 8˝ larger than the tops.
- The backing yardage is generously calculated for the minimum number of seams. Recalculate if you want to save your pennies for more "front" fabric.
- I like to piece most of the scraps and leftovers from the front of a project into the backing. To see a tutorial on making a scrappy pieced back, go to huntersdesignstudio.com > May 2012 > Tutorial – Pieced Backs.

A Few Words on Pressing

- Press at every step.
- Use a dry iron when pressing the blocks with the paper still attached.
- Press the seams away from the letter blocks unless instructed otherwise. (Sometimes a seam has a mind of its own and just doesn't want to get pressed in a specific direction. I usually let these seams win the fight, as they seem to lie flatter.)
- Paper piecing can leave bias edges on your blocks. A light spritz of starch or sizing can help keep these blocks square as you sew them into the quilt top.
- When in doubt, press!

And Finally … a Few Words about Quilting!

- Don't let your quilts stall when it's time for quilting. Remember, it's not a quilt until it's quilted!
- Feeling intimidated? Pick up some basics in books such as *First Steps to Free-Motion Quilting* by Christina Cameli (from Stash Books).
- It is perfectly acceptable to pay another artist to quilt for you.
- Don't be intimidated by the prevalence of the really intense and detailed quilting you might see on some of today's quilts. There is no rule that says this is the only kind of quilting that is acceptable. Super-dense quilting can be beautiful—but so can simple straight lines that echo the design elements from the top. That's mostly how I do it.
- Know the limits of the batting you're using. Some battings require quilt lines no more than 3˝ apart, while others can go up to 9˝. When in doubt, choose the roomier batting and over-quilt it rather than choosing the tighter batting and risk having it ball up in big spaces.
- Consider the function of the quilt. The denser the quilting, the stiffer it can be. If you want the quilt to be soft and snuggly, leave a little breathing room in the quilting. However, a quilt that is more densely quilted will wear better in the long run because the fabric has less opportunity to shift. Choose your quilting design by balancing the longevity you hope for with the snuggle factor.
- Like most skills in life, the more you practice quilting, the better you get. So make more quilts!

How to PAPER PIECE

All the characters in this book are constructed on paper foundations in the technique known as *foundation piecing* or *paper piecing*. There are many different ways to do this and many different tools and products that help make paper piecing easy to understand and simple to do.

Why Paper Piecing?

Paper piecing is a wonderful technique for accurately assembling small pieces into complex blocks, using nothing more than simple straight seams. It also kicks the need to make fiddly templates to the curb! Rather than drafting small pieces, then making templates, then drafting those onto fabric, and then cutting and piecing them together (whew!), a single piece of inexpensive paper supports the block and allows you to sew it with pin-point accuracy.

Paper piecing uses a little more fabric than traditional piecing, but you get both accuracy and ease of construction in exchange for an extra strip or two of cloth. The payoff is well worth it.

There are many great books on paper piecing, as well as numerous videos on the Internet. Most people develop their own hybrid style to construct paper-pieced blocks, so feel free to adopt what works for you and leave behind what doesn't. What follows is how I do it, along with the products and tools I like best.

Psst . . . I'll let you in on a secret: There's no such thing as the Quilt Police, so go ahead and do it your own way!

 tip *Type "paper-piecing tutorial" into your favorite Internet search engine and follow a few links to see different techniques. I recommend brewing a cup of tea and watching a few video tutorials. Then you'll be ready for the hands-on Paper-Piecing Tutorial (page 15).*

How to Make a Paper-Pieced Block

SET UP YOUR MACHINE

Every project starts with getting your machine ready to sew. Paper piecing can create extra lint, so begin by giving your machine a quick cleaning and dusting, and take care of the dust bunnies in the bobbin case!

Use a clear or open-toe foot on your machine, which will allow you to see both the needle and the sewing line easily.

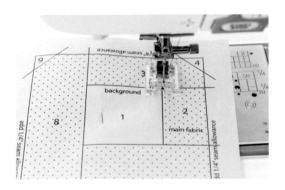

In general, use a new needle for each project (or after approximately eight hours of sewing time). Changing the needle regularly is like changing the oil in your car—it prolongs the life of your machine. Paper dulls needles quickly, so it's best to change the needle after completing a paper-piecing project. Some sources recommend using a larger needle, such as a 90/14, for paper piecing, but I find an 80/12 works great when set with a small stitch length, and it doesn't punch larger holes into the fabric.

tip

If you are going to put precious time into your projects, make sure they last by using the highest-quality products you can afford. Old or discount thread can leave you (and your quilt) in pieces!

Use high-quality, strong cotton thread. Rather than matching the thread to the fabric, I use gray for piecing because it's less visible in the seams. My favorite is Aurifil 50-weight Mako cotton—it's fine, it's strong, and it leaves very little lint behind.

Set your machine for a very small stitch length. The stitches should be just long enough that you can still wiggle a seam ripper between them, but no longer. The small stitch length perforates the paper, making it easier to remove. A small stitch length also prevents you from tearing out stitches when you tear off the paper.

CHOOSE YOUR PAPER

So let's start with the foundation of paper piecing—the paper. The paper's most important qualities are its thinness and its transparency. Thin paper tears off the finished block easily, and transparent or translucent paper allows you to see through it to more easily position the fabric pieces.

My two favorite papers for this job are vellum and newsprint: Simple Foundations Translucent Vellum Paper and Carol Doak's Foundation Paper (both by C&T Publishing; see Resources, page 142).

Vellum   I like that I can see through it, and I love how the crisp texture makes for easy tearing. I use vellum when I'm working with complex shapes so that I can easily see where I'm going.

Newsprint   This paper is wonderfully thin. It's semi-transparent and tears off like a dream. I use this for most of my projects.

In a pinch, lightweight copy paper will do. I recommend trying a practice block with several different papers to find your favorite before beginning a project.

COPY THE PATTERNS

All copiers are not created equal! The difference in size between a block printed on the copier in your home and one printed at an office supply store could be up to a half an inch, so be sure to print all the parts for your entire project at the same time, on the same copier.

About the Patterns

All patterns are printed as a mirror image of the finished pieced block.

Seam allowance reminder: Add ¼" seam allowance to all blocks when you trim.

Leader lines: These help you align your stitches at the correct angle at the edge of the block.

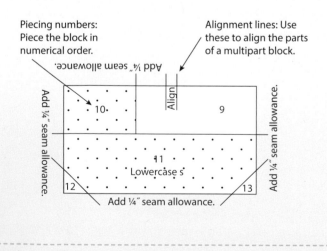

Piecing numbers: Piece the block in numerical order.

Alignment lines: Use these to align the parts of a multipart block.

REDUCING AND ENLARGING PATTERNS

Each project lists the correct height for the lettering. Copy one letter at the stated size first, and measure it to make sure that your patterns are printing out at the correct size. If not, change the copier to enlarge or reduce by 1 or 2 percent, until you have printed a perfect copy. Make a note of these settings to use for the rest of the project. For the easy formula to resize your letters for custom text, see Calculating Size Changes (page 31).

 Send any bad copies to the recycle bin immediately so they don't inadvertently sneak onto your sewing table and goof up your project.

TRIM THE PAPER

Before sewing, trim off the excess paper from each letter, leaving at least ½˝ around each block.

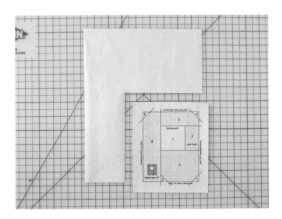

If the block is constructed in multiple sections (such as a lowercase **g**), cut the sections apart before beginning.

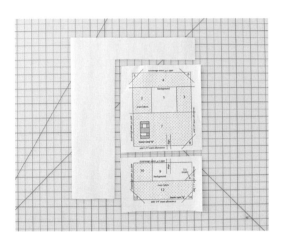

TUTORIAL PREPARATION:
Photocopy the Letter

For the paper-piecing tutorial that follows, make a copy of a lowercase **a** (pattern pullout page P2) at 200%. The block should be 5˝ tall.

PRECUT YOUR FABRIC

You can save time and fabric when paper piecing by precutting the pieces for each block. In general, each piece should be about 1˝ larger in both dimensions than its intended space: ½˝ for the ¼˝ seam allowance on each side, and another ¼˝ to ½˝ of wiggle room for aligning the piece.

If you cut your pieces only ½˝ larger, it can lead to a lot of pesky ripping and resewing to get adequate seam allowances. Having a little more fabric to play with makes for an ample seam on all sides—and less ripping out!

When piecing a lot of letters, cut strips of the most common sizes needed and cut from those to make your precut chunks. Each pattern in this book calls out the most common strip sizes needed to make the letters.

TUTORIAL PREPARATION:
Cut the Strips

Use the lowercase **a** copied at 200%.

1. Cut 1 strip 2¼˝ wide and 1 strip 3¼˝ wide from the letter fabric (teal in the photos). Cut 1 strip 2¾˝ wide from the background fabric (lime in the photos).

2. From the strips, cut chunks of fabric for each of the pieces on the paper pattern using scissors or a rotary cutter. Make sure they are at least 1˝ larger in both dimensions than the numbered areas on the pattern. Lay out the precut pieces in their approximate locations, paying attention to any directional prints in the fabric.

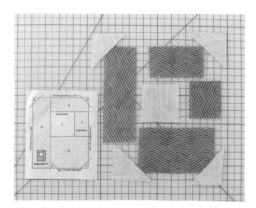

A Few Things to Note before You Sew

- Construct paper-pieced blocks in numerical order, usually from the center outward or from side to side.

- Complex patterns are split into smaller sections that will be joined after each section is pieced.

- Pin your fabric to the paper when learning to paper piece. Flat-head pins are ideal for this.

- Red thread is used in all the photos to more clearly illustrate the stitching lines.

- The printed side of the paper is visible on the back of the finished block; the right side of the fabric faces out on the unprinted side of the paper.

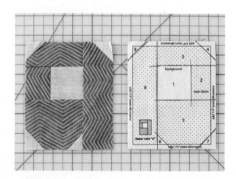

All of this will make better sense once you actually make a block!

Ready to Get Started? Here We Go!

PAPER-PIECING TUTORIAL

Use the lowercase **a** copied at 200% and the fabric strips that you previously cut.

1. Place fabric piece #1 over block area #1, on the *back* of the paper, with the right side of the fabric facing out. Hold it up to the light, looking at the printed side to make sure the fabric covers area #1 with at least a ¼″ seam allowance on all sides.

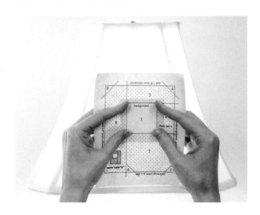

2. Pin in place using a flat-head pin.

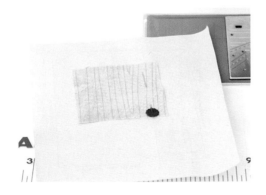

3. Place fabric piece #2 on the back of the paper, right side facing out, across area #2.

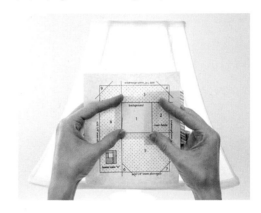

4. Imagine there is a hinge along the seam between piece #1 and piece #2. Pick up piece #2 and flip it over along the "hinge" to lay it right side down on piece #1.

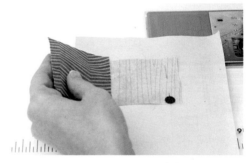

5. Position piece #2 so that there is at least a ¼″ seam allowance along the line between #1 and #2 on the paper. Hold it up to the light to check. Pin it in place, away from the sewing line.

To "test" a seam before sewing it, insert a flat-head pin along the seamline through the two pieces that make up the seam. Fold the fabric out and hold it up to the light to check it.

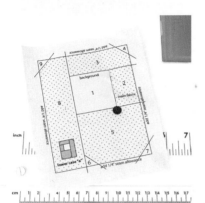

Always pin and test while you're learning to paper piece! Later, as you become more comfortable with the technique, you can abandon the pins and trust yourself to position the fabric correctly without them.

6. Place the block, fabric side down, at your machine. Position the sewing line between pieces #1 and #2 in front of the needle, so that the needle is about ¼" away from the line.

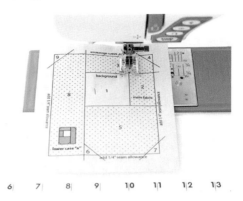

7. Begin sewing about ¼" before the sewing line. Sew on the line, sewing past the end by ¼". For sewing lines that extend to the edge of the block, sew into the seam allowance, extending the seam all the way to the edge of the paper following the printed leader lines. Remove the block from the machine and trim all the threads.

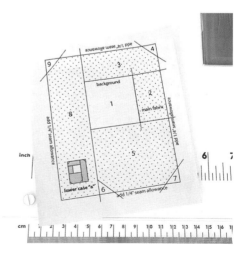

8. Turn the block so that the fabric side is up, remove the pins, and fold out piece #2. Hold it up to the light to check that it covers area #2 with an adequate seam allowance. Rip out and resew if needed.

> **tip** *When you rip out a seam in a paper-pieced block, you usually tear the paper along the seamline. Repair the tear with a small piece of clear tape on the printed side of the block.*

9. Fold piece #2 back over piece #1 and trim the seam allowance to ¼˝. You can eyeball this and cut it with a small pair of scissors.

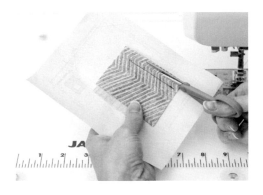

10. Flip piece #2 back into place and press. You can press with a dry iron or run your thumbnails along the seam to finger-press for speedy convenience.

11. With the fabric side of the block facing up, fold back an edge of the paper pattern to make a crease along the next seamline—in this case the seam between #1/#2 and #3. Press a good crease with your fingers. This allows you to more easily see the next seam on the unmarked side of the paper.

12. Open out the block and keep an eye on the crease. This will be the next sewing line.

13. Place piece #3 across the crease, positioning it about ¼˝ over the crease for the seam allowance.

14. Holding piece #3 in place (or pinning it), flip the block over and sew along the line for piece #3.

15. Flip, trim, and press the seam.

16. Repeat Steps 11–15 for each piece of fabric to construct the block in numerical order. Pay attention to the numbers or you might skip a piece. For example, #6 on **a** is easy to miss.

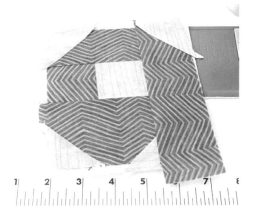

17. Press the block carefully before trimming it, giving it a light spritz of spray starch or sizing for stability. Check that all the pieces around the edges of the block have adequate coverage and that there is enough fabric for the ¼˝ seam allowance all around the block.

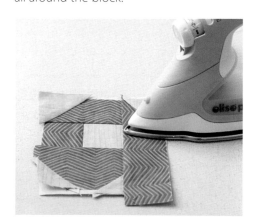

TRIM THE BLOCKS

The patterns don't have an outer ¼″ cutting line because the line would change with any enlargements or reductions.

1. Trim the sewn blocks ¼″ outside the block line using a rotary cutter, ruler, and mat to add the seam allowance. The patterns have "add ¼″ seam allowance" printed along the edges to remind you.

2. Trim all 4 sides to finish the block.

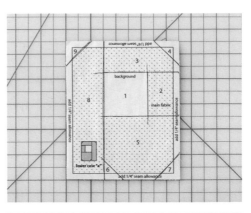

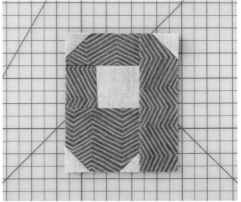

tip *The foundation paper will quickly dull your rotary blade, so keep an extra rotary cutter on hand for cutting paper-pieced blocks. Mark the handle with a label to indicate that it is your "paper" cutter. This allows you to keep your dedicated fabric cutter in sharp shape!*

MAKING BLOCKS WITH MULTIPLE SECTIONS

1. When you make a block with more than one section, piece each section and then trim the sections.

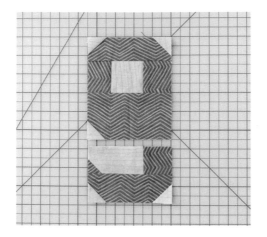

2. Pin the sections together, aligning the registration marks.

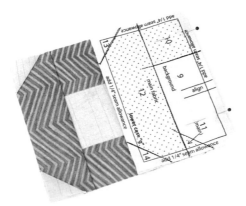

3. Sew carefully along the line through the layers from edge to edge, including the seam allowances at the beginning and end.

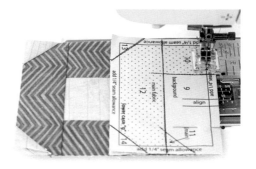

> **tip** *To avoid breaking a needle, slow down when sewing across thick seam intersections.*

4. Check that the block is constructed correctly and then tear out the paper in the seam allowance of the joined seam. Press the block open and re-press the entire block.

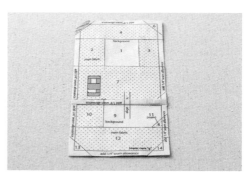

REMOVE THE PAPER

Once you have made all the blocks, it's time to remove the paper! I recommend pinching the paper on one side of a seam with your thumbnail at the edge and tearing the paper down the other side of the seam. Holding the edge like this prevents the stitches at the edge of the block from coming undone.

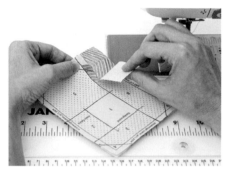

Use tweezers and pull gently at any stubborn scraps of paper that remain.

Press the blocks one more time if needed.

HOW TO PIECE ODD ANGLES

Some of the blocks have sections that are oddly shaped (for example, the diagonal legs of **K** and **R**). In general, cut the fabric for these pieces at least 1˝ larger than you would a simple rectangle—so at least 2˝ larger than the numbered space. This makes sure the section is covered on the first try and keeps you away from your seam ripper!

SETTING LETTERS INTO WORDS

All the projects include complete instructions to set the letters into words and words into word blocks. If you are designing custom text, refer to the instructions in Designing Custom Text (page 30).

 Workflow Hints

These tips will help you keep all the parts organized while making words:

■ *Always precut fabric for at least one letter at a time; stack the pieces on top of each paper letter pattern.*

■ *Group letters into words, and keep each word in a plastic zipper bag as you work.*

■ *If you are making several sizes of letters, make the largest ones first and work toward the smallest. This will enable you to use the scraps from larger letters to make the smaller ones before cutting more strips.*

■ *Use labels liberally when cutting out lots of pieces! Sticky notes and blue painter's tape are good; they stick well, can be removed easily, and leave no sticky residue.*

■ *When possible, lay out the letters and their setting components on a design surface before sewing. This will help you keep the assembly flowing in the correct order.*

■ *Press at every stage.*

Letter and Word ANATOMY

Much of the terminology that surrounds the design of letters and text originates from the times of hand-set text and printing presses.

The terms *uppercase* and *lowercase* refer to the capital and small letters we use daily, but did you know that the terms came from the letters' position in the type case? Lowercase letters were at the bottom, closer to the typesetter, to make setting words faster.

As you navigate the project instructions, it will help to be familiar with a few other terms:

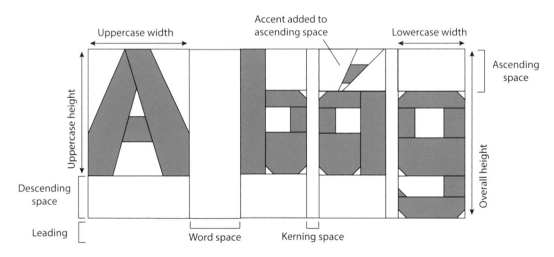

Basic anatomy of letter design

ASCENDER

This is the section of a letter that goes up, like the tail of a lowercase **b**.

DESCENDER

This is the section of a letter that goes down, like the tail of a lowercase **p**.

ASCENDING AND DESCENDING (A&D) SPACE

This is the space above and below lowercase letters that don't ascend or descend. In this book, the term *A&D strips* refers to fabric that is used to fill this space to make letters into word blocks.

KERNING (K) SPACE

Kerning is the space between letters and between words. This space can be adjusted to visually balance a word, something that modern typesetting and modern computers do automatically for us. In this book, the term *K strips* refers to fabric spacers to make letters into word blocks.

WORD SPACE

A word space is a wider kerning space that is used to space words apart.

ACCENTS

These give inflection to certain letters in words. This book includes six different accents that can be inserted into the A&D space to accommodate French and Spanish words. See *Bébé* (page 64).

LEADING

Leading is the space between the lines of text, named for the strips of lead that were used to space rows of letters for a printing press.

Choosing Fabric for LETTERS

One of the key guidelines for using lettering is to make it readable! There's little point in making a quilt full of pretty letters if they don't speak your words loud and clear—unless, of course, your intent is to convey a subtle message. Consider the following points and examples when making your fabric choices for best readability.

Concepts

When you add words to a quilt, consider your concept: which words do you want to use, and what is the point (if any) that you are trying to make? Take a look at the Gallery of Ideas (page 40). The artists used many different approaches to letter sizing and fabric contrast that offer inspiration.

Choosing the right fabric can really help the message of your words hit home. For example, check out the photo of *She Was a Nice Girl …* (page 99). I made **nice** in soft floral fabric to support the concept of a certain innocent sweetness, and I chose a broad variety of bold prints for **quilting** to make my point about how taking up quilting can add some color to a girl's life. I also changed the colors on these two words specifically for additional emphasis.

In another example, in *Leia <3s Han* (page 68), I chose a deep blue background with a pattern that resembles stars in space to support the *Star Wars* movie reference.

Whatever your concept, don't forget to have fun with the fabric choices. There are so many lovely fabrics available, with more arriving in your local quilt store every week. It would be a shame to miss out on playing with them!

How to Make the Letters Stand Out

Like most quilt patterns, these letters thrive on contrast—both value contrast (from light to dark) and pattern-scale contrast (from large-scale prints to small prints to solids). In general, each letter and its background need a certain amount of contrast to be readable. As with any rule, there is, of course, room for exceptions: low-value contrast can be used to make subtle statements in a phrase, just as high-value contrast can be used to emphasize a word.

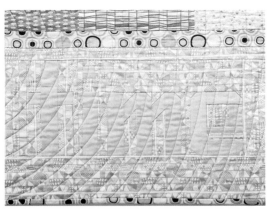

Low color-value contrast—Word blends softly with background.

High color-value contrast—Words stand out from background.

HOW TO CREATE GOOD VALUE CONTRAST

One of the best ways to analyze the color and pattern values of your fabric is to take a snapshot and then convert the image into grayscale. Use your smartphone or tablet to take the picture, and use any one of dozens of photo apps to turn the image into black and white.

The images below are from my auditions of fabric for *Love What You Do* (page 88). In these two shots, you can see that while my colors looked good in the first snapshot, the second told me that I was going to lose contrast with the purple if I used it.

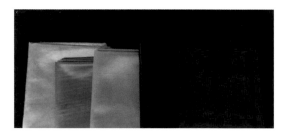
Contrast looks good in color photo.

Black-and-white photo shows that purple fabric would be "lost" against background.

Frank Sardisco, one of my beloved art professors, always used to say, "Battleship gray is the enemy of art!" He sure knew what he was talking about. The best way to make a quilt go visually flat is to choose a lot of fabrics that will appear medium gray in a black-and-white photo.

It's always smart to check the values before you cut into your fabric. Who doesn't like good value contrast! And remember … no battleship gray!

PATTERN SCALE

It's possible to use large-scale prints as long as no elements in the print share colors with the background. All the parts of a large print must contrast with its neighbors in order to be effective, and even then the choppiness of a big, busy print might defeat the readability. Remember, the first rule of lettering is to make it readable!

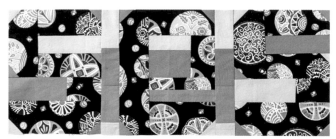
Paula Fleischer's first attempt at the letters for her quilt *Sesquipedalian* (page 47). The scale of the print was too large and choppy, and the background fabric was too dark for the letters to read effectively.

Detail from *Sesquipedalian* (page 47). Paula's revamped letters are so much more readable.

Small-scale prints work well because their overall look can create one overall value. If you are using two small-scale prints, don't use the same color in the letter fabric and background fabric, or the letters might disappear.

Detail of *Hello, Amelia!* (page 62). Prints work together because there is color-value contrast.

If you want to play it safe, consider pairing prints (especially larger-scale prints) with either a solid fabric or one that "reads" solid.

Always test your fabric combinations with a word or a few letters if you have doubts. In the following example, the print seemed to contrast well with the gray background before it was cut. Once it was pieced, the wide contrast in the flower print made it average to a gray that was similar to the background.

This resulted in the edges of the letters being fuzzy, which made it a bit too mushy in its readability for my taste—not to mention that I was flirting with the dreaded battleship gray!

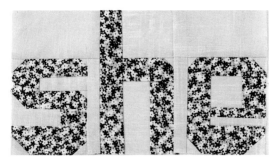

In this rejected fabric choice for *She Was a Nice Girl…* (page 92), the similarity between the value in the small print and the background made the edges of the letters fuzzy.

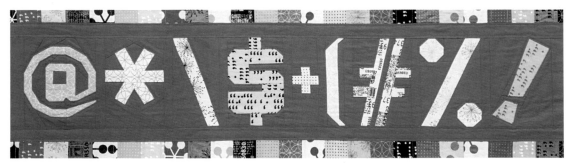

Detail from *Rackafrax!* (page 82). Large-scale prints team up with solid background.

DIRECTIONAL PRINTS

A directional print like a stripe can look playful and energetic in a letter. However, aligning the stripes or motifs within a complex letter might be far more hassle than it's worth. If keeping every stripe matched up and moving in the right direction matters to you—and you are using lots of letters with diagonals such as **k**, **r**, and **x**—take the easier road and save your stripes for big blocks and borders.

Stripes work well in simple vertical letters such as i, l, and t.

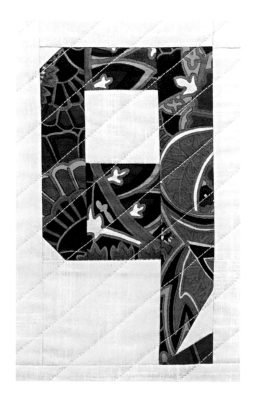

Designing Your Own QUILT

Many of the projects are designed so you can change the words to customize your quilt. Where possible, the size of the text block is given so that you can customize the text to make the project your own.

You can easily insert a line of text into any quilt design that assembles in rows, or run text around the perimeter of a quilt top. See *Life Has Its Ups and Downs* (page 48) for a fabulous example of using words in the borders.

Word Inspiration

You don't have to look far for words to use in a project. Our daily life is filled with words and phrases, and many can be fun to use in word-based projects. Following are some ideas on where to look for words to use on your quilt projects. For a list of more specific ideas and inspiration to get you started, see For My Next Project (page 51).

- **Names**   Put a name on your quilt to personalize it. Young children love this.
- **A special date or event**   A quilt can commemorate a wedding or anniversary; it can celebrate the arrival of a baby.
- **Quotes**   A little Internet research can lead you to thousands of quotes on any topic you can think of.
- **Quotes from pop culture and geek favorites**   Make a quilt for your favorite pop-culture fan based on famous quotes from movies, shows, or music.
- **Bold statements**   Deliver some advice or encouragement in quilted form.
- **Team affiliations**   Add **Go Team** to a project in club colors.

Designing Custom Text

Reducing or enlarging text requires some *simple* calculations. I know—the thought of doing math makes some of us want to swoon like a Victorian lady with a case of the vapors! But really, this is easy grade-school math, not college algebra. You'll need a calculator, but swooning isn't necessary!

Note that although all the project instructions give measurements in fractions so that they are easier to find on a quilting ruler, decimals are used for the calculations. I have rounded many fractions in the project measurements that are smaller than 1/8″ because anything less is just too persnickety to deal with (or see) on a ruler. Also, these tiny measurements amount to just a thread or two in terms of fabric and can often be eased or stretched as needed with a little steam from your iron. There are also several cases in which you will cut a piece a tiny bit larger than needed and then trim it to fit the letters next to it.

Once you make the calculations and reduce or enlarge your patterns, you're done dealing with any weird numbers. When you paper piece, no matter what size your pattern, you still precut simple chunks of fabric for sewing.

 Fractions to Decimals

Use this handy chart for fraction-to-decimal conversions and vice versa.

Fraction	Decimal equivalent
1/8	0.125
1/4	0.25
3/8	0.375
1/2	0.5
5/8	0.625
3/4	0.75
7/8	0.875

ARRANGING YOUR TEXT

Once you've decided on the words you want to use, make some copies of the Alphabet Worksheets (page 36) and cut out the letters. Play with these to design the layout of your text.

In general, when there is a lot of text, a mixture of upper- and lowercase letters is easier to read (just like reading this sentence). Sometimes switching to all capitals allows for easier construction because there's no A&D space to manage. However, all uppercase can be harder to read and might look like you're SHOUTING YOUR CONCEPT!

When you plan to fit words into a space, remember to leave a little room at the edges. If you have a 24″ opening, make the text fit in about 20″, so that the letters breathe in their space and don't merge with the edges.

In the following tutorial, **Go to sleep!** *and* **GO TO SLEEP!**
are used as examples. We'll size the words to fit a space of 20˝.

When possible, leave at least 1˝ finished space above the word for good visual balance. If you have ascenders and descenders, the text will look best centered vertically. In cases where there are no ascenders or descenders, you may want to reduce the height of the word space by an inch or two. This keeps it from "swimming" in the space. In *Hello, Amelia!* (page 62), I took 1½˝ off the bottom of both words.

CALCULATING SIZE CHANGES

1. Calculate the finished length of the word(s) at 100% by adding the widths of all the letters, plus K strips and word spaces. Use the handy charts (page 39) for dimensions of letters, numbers, punctuation, and symbols, as well as space to allow for K strips (0.375˝ wide), A&D space (1.25˝ high), and word spaces (1.5˝ wide).

In the **Go to sleep!** example, the calculations are as follows:

Go	**G** + (k) + **o** 3 + 0.375 + 2 = 5.375˝
to	**t** + (k) + **o** 1.75 + 0.375 + 2 = 4.125˝
sleep!	**s** + (k) + **l** + (k) + **e** + (k) + **e** + (k) + **p** + (k) + **!** 2 + 0.375 + 0.625 + 0.375 + 2 + 0.375 + 2 + 0.375 + 2 + 0.375 + 1 = 11.5˝
Word spaces	We need 2 word spaces, 1.5˝ each.
FINAL CALCULATION	5.375 + 1.5 + 4.125 + 1.5 + 11.5 = 24˝

Now that you know how to do the calculations, I'll just tell you that for **GO TO SLEEP!** the final calculation is 33.625˝.

2. Determine the height of the word, again referring to the charts (page 39).

If you are using a mixture of letters with both ascenders and descenders, as in **Go to sleep!**, the height is 5˝.

If you are using all capital letters, as in **GO TO SLEEP!**, the height is 3¾˝.

If you are using a mixture of letters that have no descenders, as in my name, **Sam**, the height is 3¾˝.

If you are using all lowercase letters with no ascenders or descenders, as in **some**, the height is 2½˝.

3. Determine how much you should enlarge or reduce the patterns to make the letters fit your quilt. You'll need to perform some simple calculations in which

D = the desired length or height of the space in your quilt,

F = the length of the word or phrase with spacing at full size (100%), and

M = the multiplier, or the percentage to reduce or enlarge the pattern to fit your space.

D ÷ F = M: Do the calculation with the length first, as that's usually the more important measurement to fit.

Go to sleep!	D = 20 F = 24 M = 20 ÷ 24 = 83.33%. I recommend rounding to 80%. If you print the letters at 80%, **G** is 3″ tall, and **o** is 2″ tall.
GO TO SLEEP!	D = 20 F = 33.625 M = 20 ÷ 33.625 = 59.48%. I recommend rounding to 60%. If you print these letters at 60%, **G** is 2.25″ tall.

In both cases, these letters will be easy to make in terms of size. The choice of mixed letters or all capitals is driven by your aesthetic opinion and concept rather than difficult sizing. If the height of the space is in question, the all-capital version is shorter than the mixed version because it has no descenders.

If you want to make **GO TO SLEEP!** fit a 40″ space instead of a 20″ space, just change the value for D to 40:

GO TO SLEEP!	D = 40 F = 33.625 M = 40 ÷ 33.625 = 118.95%. I recommend rounding to 120%. If you print these letters at 120%, **G** is 4.5″ tall, and **o** is 2.4″ tall.

4. Reduce or enlarge the spacing. K strips and word spaces also need to be reduced or enlarged by the same percentage as the letters.

Go to sleep!	At 100%, the K strip is 0.375″: 0.375″ × 0.80 = 0.3″. Since 0.3″ is an awkward measurement to find on a ruler, I recommend rounding down to 0.25″ (¼″) or up to 0.375″ (⅜″). The word space is 1.5″: 1.5″ × 0.80 = 1.2″. Again, 1.2″ is awkward on a ruler, so I recommend rounding up to 1.25″ (1¼″).
GO TO SLEEP!	The K strip is 0.375″: 0.375″ × 0.60 = 0.225″. 0.225″ is an awkward measurement to find on a ruler, so I recommend rounding up to 0.25″ (¼″). The word space is 1.5″: 1.5″ × 0.60 = 0.9″. Again, 0.9″ is awkward on a ruler, so I recommend rounding down to 0.875″ (⅞″) or rounding up to 1″.

note

When you cut K strips and word spaces, be sure to add a ½″ seam allowance (¼″ for each side of the strip) to the measurements that you calculate above.

SPECIAL TIPS FOR SMALL OR LARGE TEXT

During the creation of this book, the gallery artists and I made letters in all sizes, from 40% reduction to 480% enlargement!

Small Text

When making the smallest letters (anything under 50%), consider these points:

- You might have to make two copies of a letter that has multiple parts so that you have adequate paper around each section.
- When calculating the width of K strips, make them no smaller than ¼″ finished (¾″ cut). Anything less is a pain in the patootie to piece with a decent ¼″ seam allowance.
- When precutting fabric for small letters, don't go too small. It's easier to cut off a bigger chunk of waste fabric than it is to keep your grip on a small one.
- When sewing on the triangle corners that give the letters their roundness, sew just to the left of the stitching line to make the triangle a thread or two larger. This makes the small letters easier to read.
- Fiddling with small things can get the better of your patience. Just take it slowly and it will all come together just fine! Adding chocolate to the sewing session helps too.
- Small letters are quite adorable and worth the effort.

Large Text

When making large letters (anything larger than the size of the paper), consider these points:

- Add additional marks to the pattern to help you line up multiple sheets once the letters are copied.
- When you need to join pattern pieces together, use clear tape across the entire join. This prevents the presser foot from getting hung up on paper between gaps in the tape.
- Pin generously on large pieces to prevent shifting while you are sewing.

CALCULATING FABRIC REQUIREMENTS

A ¼-yard piece each of letter fabric and background fabric will make approximately 8 to 12 letters at 100%, depending on the complexity and the mix of upper- and lowercase letters you use. You can use either a fat quarter (18″ × 21″) or a ¼-yard cut (9″ × 42″). The background includes the fabric that fills out the letters to create the letter blocks.

Uppercase letters need more letter fabric, and lowercase letters need more background. Likewise, a line containing several lowercase **i** blocks takes far less fabric than a similar number of uppercase **S** blocks.

It's not an exact science, so when in doubt, *buy extra fabric*. You can always piece your leftovers into the backing. You can also peruse the yardages listed in the various projects to help you come up with a good estimate.

SETTING LETTERS INTO WORDS AND WORD BLOCKS

Once you have made the letters, it's time to turn them into words. One way to do it (and the simplest in terms of the math) is to make single A&D strips, K strips, and word spaces for each letter. *The example shows a smaller phrase so that you can better see the spaces:*

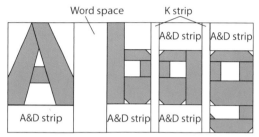

Connect letters with A&D strips, K strips, and word spaces.

However, with just a little more planning, you can combine these spaces for efficiency, saving a little fabric and time:

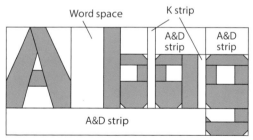

A&D strips and K strips reorganized for faster piecing and less fabric use

The combined version is used in all the projects in this book. I did all the calculations for you!

There are two ways to calculate the combined spaces:

1. **Mathematically** Add the calculated size of the letters and K strips together, add the seam allowance, and use the result.

2. **Physically** Place the sections on your mat, measure the spaces, and then add seam allowances as needed. You can always add a larger piece and trim it back later.

The first version ensures accuracy and will keep your quilt top flatter, but the second version is fine if you have relatively accurate piecing skills. I always do the math first and then check it against the mat before I cut to see if I made a mistake.

LEADING

Once the words and phrases are set into blocks, they must be set apart in lines by leading space. In the printing world, leading is always the same height, regardless of the presence of descenders. However, here you have the option to play aesthetically with how far to set the lines of text apart to create a visual balance that you like. You might also need to squeeze this space to fit all your text into the space available.

I recommend putting the text on a design wall and testing strips that range from 10% to 40% as high as the tallest letter to get the perfect balance. You can also mix up the sizes as needed or as desired. See *She Just Ignored People* (page 100) for an example using several sizes of text.

Life Has Its Ups and Downs, 66″ × 93″
Designed, pieced, and quilted by Vicki Tymczyszyn, 2013

Vicki added text borders to classic chevrons.

BE Amazing, 72″ × 92″
Designed, pieced, and quilted by Sam Hunter, 2013

Twenty-eight encouraging words to go and be every day—
one for every letter of the alphabet (and a couple of spares)!

I Must Have Flowers, 91½˝ × 106½˝
Designed, pieced, and bound by Sam Hunter
and quilted by Lisa Alexakis, 2013

This quilt features fabrics from the Always Blooming
collection by Susy Pilgrim Waters for P&B Textiles.

For My Next Project...

Inspired by quilts that have something to say, my friends and I already have ideas for our next quilts, as well as other smaller but oh-so-clever projects!

- A two-part sign for the sewing room door. The top will say **THE QUILTER IS**. The bottom one, attached by a ribbon, will say **IN** on one side and **OUT** on the other.

- A back-to-back door sign with **GO AWAY** on one side and **COME IN** on the other

- An initialized e-reader or tablet cover

- Quilted appliance covers for the kitchen: **MIX IT UP** for the mixer and **WAKE UP** for the coffeemaker

- A **Do Not Disturb** door hanger

- A **Go Away** eye mask

- A quilt with wedding or anniversary dates and maybe the couple's names

- A retirement quilt with the person's name and/or favorite catchphrase

- Rah-rah team quilts:

  Go Mizzou, in black and gold with tiger print fabric

  Hit 'em hard, every yard! ISU

  Go, Dodgers!

  Rise and Shout, the Cougars Are Out

  I'm a Jayhawk

- Favorite quotes:

  For the reader who relishes the rainy day when she curls up in her favorite chair with a good book: **A book is a dream you hold in your hand. —Neil Gaiman**

  For my girl headed to college: **Nothing is impossible; the word itself says "I'm possible"! —Audrey Hepburn**

  A hug is a great gift—one size fits all, and it's easy to exchange.

- **Couch Potato** on a lap throw will make a good gift for a certain guy.

- Favorite movie quote for a couch quilt—one for each member of the family!

  I'll have what she's having.

  There's no place like home.

  Is this heaven? No, Iowa.

  There's no crying in baseball.

  Hakuna Matata

  My precious

- **Bon Appétit** on place mats or a table runner.

- A growth chart with the child's name on it as well as numbers.

- A play mat for the grandbaby—with numbers

- A signature quilt for someone coming or leaving home—**Welcome Home** or **We'll Miss You** paper pieced in big letters but leaving plenty of room for signatures.

- Bunting with the letters spelling a name or a celebration, such as **Happy Birthday!**

What about you? What will be your signature piece? What is your quilt going to say?

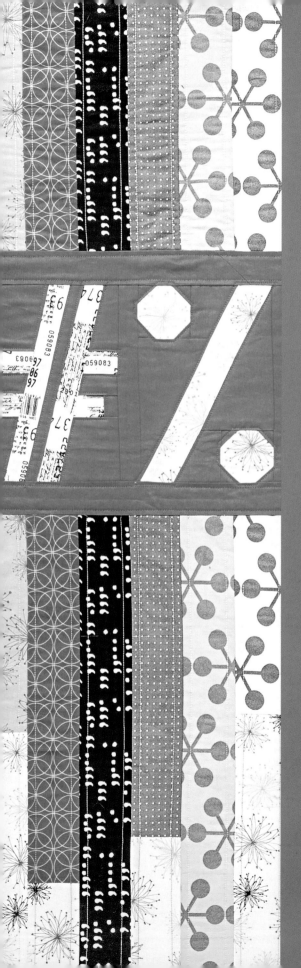

P
R
O
J
E
C
T
S

Good news! A little one is coming ... or a little one is here. There are gifts to make and showers to attend. Quilters, let's wrap the new arrival in fabric; it's our instinct, is it not? Let's celebrate life! Welcome, sweet child!

Welcome, Baby!

Finished baby quilt: 40¾″ × 49¾″ Designed, pieced, and quilted by Sam Hunter, 2013

✳ GO SHOPPING!

- **Quilt center:** ⅞ yard light print or 12 squares 9½″ × 9½″

- **Letters:** ⅝ yard light print

- **Letter background:** 1½ yards green (1¾ yards if using for heart background also)

- **Inner border:** ¼ yard contrasting print

- **Corner square** (*if not making heart*): 12½″ × 12½″ coordinating print

- **Heart background** (*if different from letter background*): 1 fat quarter or ⅓ yard coordinating print

- **Cornerstone:** Scrap, at least 1¾″ × 1¾″, of contrasting print

- **Binding:** ½ yard

- **Backing:** 2¾ yards

- **Batting:** 49″ × 58″

This quilt features fabrics from the Precious collection by Another Point of View for Windham Fabrics and the Many Eyes Looking collection by Andover Fabrics.

✳ note

This project includes three variations. Read through to the end to see all the possibilities before choosing the words you want to make.

Print the Patterns

For the patterns, refer to the pullout. To adjust the printing, if necessary, refer to Reducing and Enlarging Patterns (page 13).

Choose the words you wish to make, and print the letters at 200% (the lowercase **e** is 5″ tall).

Paste a sticky note over the instructions that you aren't using so that you don't inadvertently follow them!

Make the Letters

For sewing techniques, refer to How to Paper Piece (page 10).

1. Cut 1 strip × width of fabric for each strip size to start. Cut more as needed.
   - Letters: 2¼″, 3¼″
   - Background: 2½″, 3½″

2. Paper piece the letters.

3. Press, trim, and remove the paper.

The short and long words use some of the same strip sizes, so check your leftovers before cutting new strips.

make it yours

Before collecting your fabrics, choose the layout.

For the quilt center, you can use just one fabric or a simple grid of coordinating squares. Packs of precut 10″ squares are great for this, and you can use leftover squares to make a pieced backing.

For the corner square, use just one fabric or piece the heart.

You can use the words in this chapter or personalize the quilt with a name.

When designing a personalized word or phrase, give the letters a couple of inches of breathing room.

The short word block is 27″ wide finished, so design your word to be no longer than 25″.

The long word block is 36″ finished, so design your word to be no longer than 34″. Add fabric to each side of the word blocks until you reach the unfinished length of each.

To design and print your words at the correct size, refer to Designing Custom Text (page 30) and Reducing and Enlarging Patterns (page 13).

You can center the words or move one or both toward one end to anchor them at the corner. See *Hello, Amelia!* (page 62).

You can also move a border to the opposite side to make the words read correctly. See the difference in layout in *Welcome, Baby!* (page 61) and *Hello, Amelia!*

If you have no descenders in either word space, reduce the height of the word space and re-center the word vertically. In *Hello, Amelia!* I took 1½″ off the bottom of both words.

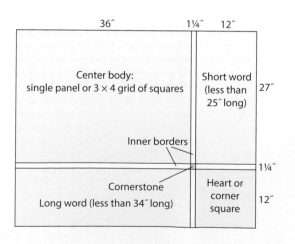

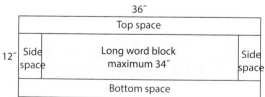

Make the Words

SHORT WORD: **baby**

1. From letter background fabric:
   - Cut 1 strip 3″ × width of fabric.
     Subcut 2 rectangles 3″ × 4½″ (A).
     Subcut 1 rectangle 3″ × 14¾″ (C).

   - Cut 1 strip 1¼″ × width of fabric.
     Subcut 3 rectangles 1¼″ × 8″ (B).

   - Cut 1 strip 4⅞″ × width of fabric.
     Subcut 2 rectangles 4⅞″ × 10½″ (D).

   - Cut 2 strips 1½″ × width of fabric.
     Subcut 2 strips 1½″ × 27½″ (E).

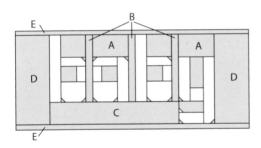

2. Sew A pieces to the top of **a** and **y**.

3. Sew B strips between **b**, **a**, and **b** and to the right side of the second **b**.

4. Sew piece C to the bottom of **bab**.

5. Sew **y** to the right side of **bab**.

6. Sew a D piece to each side of **baby**.

7. Sew E strips to the top and bottom of **baby**.

SHORT WORD: **time**

1. From letter background fabric:
   - Cut 1 strip 1¼″ × width of fabric.
     Subcut 1 strip 1¼″ × 8″ (A).
     Subcut 2 strips 1¼″ × 5½″ (B).

   - Cut 1 strip 3″ × width of fabric.
     Subcut 1 rectangle 3″ × 11¾″ (C).

   - Cut 1 strip 5⅝″ × width of fabric.
     Subcut 2 rectangles 5⅝″ × 8″ (D).

   - Cut 1 strip 4″ × width of fabric.
     Subcut 1 strip 4″ × 27½″ (E).

   - Cut 1 strip 1½″ × width of fabric.
     Subcut 1 strip 1½″ × 27½″ (F).

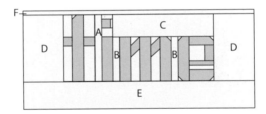

2. Sew strip A between **t** and **i**.

3. Sew B strips to the left side of **m** and between **m** and **e**.

4. Sew piece C to the top of **me**.

5. Sew **ti** to **me**.

6. Sew a D piece to each side of **time**.

7. Sew strip E to the bottom of **time** and strip F to the top.

SHORT WORD: **hello**

1. From letter background fabric:
   - Cut 1 strip 3″ × width of fabric.
     Subcut 2 rectangles 3″ × 4½″ (A).

   - Cut 1 strip 1¼″ × width of fabric.
     Subcut 4 rectangles 1¼″ × 8″ (B).

   - Cut 1 strip 8″ × width of fabric.
     Subcut 1 rectangle 8″ × 2½″ (C).
     Subcut 1 square 8″ × 8″ (D).

   - Cut 1 strip 4″ × width of fabric.
     Subcut 1 strip 4″ × 27½″ (E).*

   - Cut 1 strip 1½″ × width of fabric.
     Subcut 1 strip 1½″ × 27½″ (F).

I trimmed piece E on Hello, Amelia! (page 62) to 2½″ because there were no descenders on either word.

❋ note

*If you want to put **hello** on the long side of the quilt, use the following measurements.*

D: Cut 1 rectangle 8″ × 17″.
E: Cut 1 strip 4″ × 36½″.
F: Cut 1 strip 1½″ × 36½″.

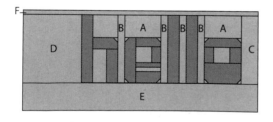

2. Sew A pieces to the top of **e** and **o**.

3. Sew B strips between **h**, **e**, **l**, **l**, and **o**.

4. Sew piece C to the right side of **hello**.

5. Sew piece D to left side of **hello**.

6. Sew strip E to the bottom of **hello** and strip F to the top.

LONG WORD: **welcome**

1. From letter background fabric:
   - Cut 1 strip 1¼″ × width of fabric.
     Subcut 6 strips 1¼″ × 5½″ (A).

   - Cut 1 strip 3″ × width of fabric.
     Subcut 1 rectangle 3″ × 11¾″ (B).
     Subcut 1 rectangle 3″ × 21¼″ (C).

   - Cut 1 strip 1⅞″ × width of fabric.
     Subcut 2 rectangles 1⅞″ × 8″ (D).

   - Cut 1 strip 4″ × width of fabric.
     Subcut 1 strip 4″ × 36½″ (E).

   - Cut 1 strip 1½″ × width of fabric.
     Subcut 1 strip 1½″ × 36½″ (F).

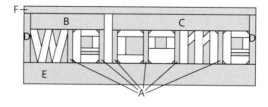

2. Sew A strips between **w** and **e** and to the right side of that first **e**.

3. Sew A strips to the left side of **c** and between **c**, **o**, **m**, and **e**.

4. Sew piece B to the top of **we**.

5. Sew piece C to the top of **come**.

6. Sew **I** between **we** and **come**.

7. Sew a D piece to each side of **welcome**.

8. Sew strip E to the bottom of **welcome** and strip F to the top.

LONG WORD: **snuggle**

1. From letter background fabric:
- Cut 2 strips 3″ × width of fabric.
  Subcut 2 rectangles 3″ × 4½″ (A).
  Subcut 1 rectangle 3″ × 1¾″ (B).
  Subcut 1 rectangle 3″ × 14¾″ (F).
  Subcut 1 rectangle 3″ × 23½″ (G).

- Cut 2 strips 1¼″ × width of fabric.
  Subcut 3 rectangles 1¼″ × 5½″ (C).
  Subcut 1 rectangle 1¼″ × 8″ (D).
  Subcut 2 rectangles 1¼″ × 10½″ (E).

- Cut 1 strip 3⅝″ × width of fabric.
  Subcut 2 rectangles 3⅝″ × 10½″ (H).

- Cut 2 strips 1½″ × width of fabric.
  Subcut 2 rectangles 1½″ × 36½″ (J).

2. Sew A pieces to the top and bottom of **e**.

3. Sew piece B to the bottom of **l**.

4. Sew C strips between **s**, **n**, and **u** and to the right side of **u**.

5. Sew strip D between **g** and **g**.

6. Sew E strips to the left side of **l** and between **l** and **e**.

7. Sew piece F to the bottom of **snu**.

8. Sew **snu** to **gg**.

9. Sew piece G to the top of **snugg**.

10. Sew **snugg** to **le**.

11. Sew an H piece to each side of **snuggle**.

12. Sew J strips to the top and bottom of **snuggle**.

Make the Heart Corner Square

1. Copy the heart pattern at 200%.

2. From the heart background fabric:
   - Cut 1 square 9″ × 9″ and cut in half once on the diagonal to make 2 triangles.
   - Cut 1 square 8″ × 8″ and cut in half once on the diagonal to make 2 triangles.

3. Piece the heart from a selection of your lettering scraps and the remainder of the heart background fabric.

4. Press, trim, and remove the paper.

5. Sew 9″ triangles to the right and left sides of the heart, matching the center of each triangle to the center of each side. Trim off the excess tip of each triangle to align with the sides.

6. Sew 8″ triangles to the top and bottom of the heart, matching the centers.

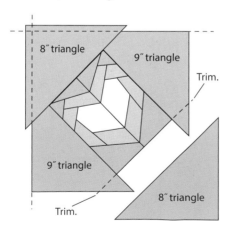

7. Trim the block to 12½″ × 12½″.

Put It Together

1. From quilt center fabric:
   - Cut 1 rectangle 27½″ × 36½″.
     Or sew together 12 squares 9½″ × 9½″ into a 3 × 4 grid.

2. From inner border fabric:
   - Cut 3 strips 1¾″ × width of fabric.
     Subcut 1 strip 1¾″ × 36½″.
     Subcut 1 strip 1¾″ × 27½″.
     Subcut 2 strips 1¾″ × 12½″.

3. From scraps:
   - Cut 1 cornerstone 1¾″ × 1¾″.

4. Sew the quilt together, referring to the quilt assembly diagram or using the arrangement of your choice.

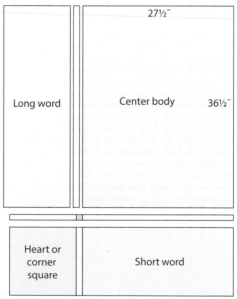

Quilt assembly

Welcome, Baby!, 40¾″ × 49¾″

Hello, Amelia! 39¼″ × 48¼″
Designed, pieced, and quilted by Sam Hunter, 2013

This quilt features fabrics from
the Wrens and Friends collection
by Gina Martin for Moda Fabrics.

Detail of *Hello, Amelia!*

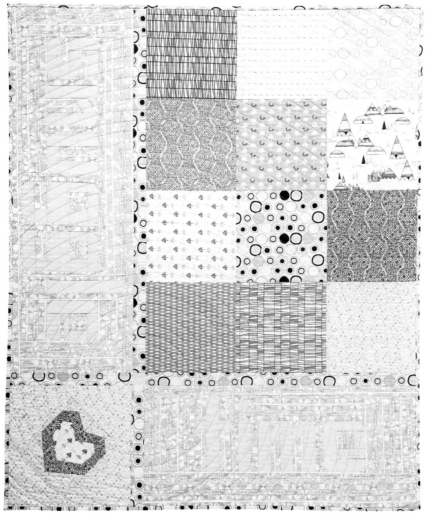

Snuggle Time, 40¾˝ × 49¾˝
Designed, pieced, and quilted by Sam Hunter, 2013

This quilt features fabrics from the Indian Summer collection by Sarah Watson for Art Gallery Fabrics and Kona Cotton Solids by Robert Kaufman Fabrics.

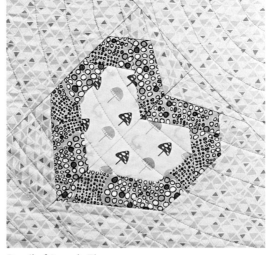

Detail of *Snuggle Time*

I love using squares in designs. Their perfect symmetry is both inspiring and comforting. Think baby blocks. Think simple shapes in simple colors. Think global. *Baby*—a sweet word in any language.

Bébé

Finished wallhanging: 33" × 11½"

Designed, pieced, and quilted by Sam Hunter, 2013

✳ GO SHOPPING!

- **Quilt body light:**
  ⅓ yard pale gray

- **Quilt body medium:**
  ⅓ yard sage

- **Accent:** Scraps or a charm square of teal print

- **Binding:** ⅓ yard

- **Backing:** ⅔ yard

- **Batting:** 41" × 20"

This quilt features fabrics from the Painter's Canvas collection by Laura Gunn for Michael Miller Fabrics and Kona Cotton Solids by Robert Kaufman Fabrics.

Print the Patterns

For the letter patterns, refer to the pullout. For the accents, refer to Patterns (page 136). To adjust the printing, if necessary, refer to Reducing and Enlarging Patterns (page 13).

Print the following patterns at 120% (the lowercase **b** is 4½" tall):

- Lowercase: **b** (2), **e** (2)
- Accents: ´ (acute accent) (1 or 2)

✳ note

The French word for baby *is* bébé; *the Spanish is* bebé.

Precut the Setting Sections

To make the most efficient use of your fabric, cut the block setting sections before you make the letters.

1. From light fabric, cut and set aside the following:

   - Cut 1 strip 7⅝" × width of fabric.
     Subcut 5 rectangles 7⅝" × 2½" (A).
     Subcut and trim 4 rectangles 7½" × 2⅞" (B).
     Subcut and trim 4 rectangles 2⅞" × 1¾" (C).
     Subcut and trim 2 squares 2½" × 2½" (D).

2. From medium fabric, cut the following and set aside for the block setting sections:

   - Cut 1 strip 7⅝" × width of fabric.
     Subcut 5 rectangles 7⅝" × 2½" (E).
     Subcut and trim 4 rectangles 7½" × 2⅞" (F).
     Subcut and trim 4 rectangles 2⅞" × 1¾" (G).
     Subcut and trim 2 squares 2½" × 2½" (H).

Spell a name in the blocks by creating one block per letter. For a long name, such as Rosemary, or for a first and middle name, consider stacking the letters into two rows and adding a heart block if you need to fill space.

To design and print your words at the correct size, refer to Designing Custom Text (page 30) and Reducing and Enlarging Patterns (page 13).

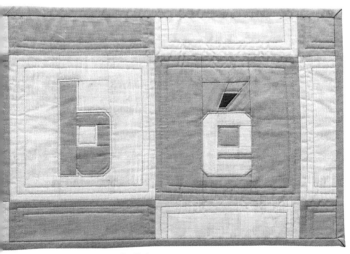

Detail of *Bébé*

Make the Letters

For sewing techniques, refer to How to Paper Piece (page 10).

1. Start with leftovers from cutting the block setting sections. When you need more strips, cut one at a time in the strip widths listed.

   - Light fabric: 1¾″, 2½″
   - Medium fabric: 1¾″, 2½″

2. Paper piece the letters and accents.

3. Press, trim, and remove the paper.

Make the Word

b BLOCKS

1. Sew C pieces to the top and bottom of **b**.

2. Sew a B piece to each side of **b**.

3. Sew E pieces to the top and bottom of **b**.

4. Repeat to make 2 **b** blocks.

é BLOCKS

1. Sew an accent to the top of **e**.

2. Sew G pieces to the top and bottom of **é**.

3. Sew an F piece to each side of **é**.

4. Sew A pieces to the top and bottom of **é**.

5. Repeat to make 2 **é** blocks.

Put It Together

1. Sew the letter blocks together in the correct order.

2. Sew D squares to both ends of the remaining E piece.

3. Sew the D/E unit to the left side of the first **b**.

4. Sew H squares to both ends of the remaining A piece.

5. Sew the H/A unit to the right side of the second **é**.

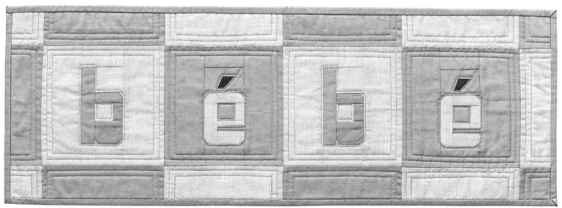

Quilt assembly

Bébé, 33″ × 11½″

A long time ago, in a galaxy far, far away ... the heroes vie for the heroine's attentions—acting up, acting out, and strutting like roosters as they fight through peril and calamity. The heroine makes her choice as the bad guys are about to do bad things to one of her suitors. In the final moments, she says it out loud: I love you. His response makes fanboy history.

Leia <3s Han

Finished quilt: 60½″ × 80½″   Designed, pieced, and quilted by Sam Hunter, 2013

❋ GO SHOPPING!

- **Background 1:**
  2 yards medium blue dot

- **Background 2:**
  2 yards dark blue dot

- **Letters:** ⅞ yard dark blue

- **Letter and word background:**
  2¼ yards platinum gray

- **Binding:** ⅝ yard dark blue dot

This quilt features fabrics from the Quilter's Linen and Quilter's Linen Dots collections by Robert Kaufman Fabrics.

- **Backing:** 5 yards

- **Batting:** 69″ × 89″

Print the Patterns

For the patterns, refer to the pullout. To adjust the printing, if necessary, refer to Reducing and Enlarging Patterns (page 13).

Print the following patterns at 214% (the upper-case **I** is 8″ tall; the lowercase **e** is 5⅜″ tall):

- Uppercase: **I** (2)
- Lowercase: **e, k, l, n, o** (3), **u, v, w, y**

Make the Letters

For sewing techniques, refer to How to Paper Piece (page 10).

1. Cut 1 strip × width of fabric for each strip size to start. Cut more as needed.

  - Letters: 2½″, 3½″
  - Background: 2¾″, 3¾″

2. Paper piece the letters.

3. Press, trim, and remove the paper.

- - - ‹

make it yours

When designing a personalized phrase, give the words a couple of inches of breathing room.

The talk bubbles are 25" × 36" finished, so design your word blocks to be no larger than 21" × 32".

To design and print your words at the correct size, refer to Designing Custom Text (page 30) and Reducing and Enlarging Patterns (page 13).

Cut the Setting Pieces

Cut the setting pieces for both talk bubbles at the same time. Mark the pieces with sticky notes or blue painter's tape to keep them in order. If you have a design wall, place the parts on the wall with the words as you cut.

From letter background fabric:

- Cut 2 strips 1¼" × width of fabric.
  Subcut 8 rectangles 1¼" × 5⅞" (A).

- Cut 2 strips 3⅛" × width of fabric.
  Subcut 1 rectangle 3⅛" × 15½" (B).
  Subcut 1 rectangle 3⅛" × 10½" (C).
  Subcut 1 rectangle 3⅛" × 17⅜" (D).

- Cut 2 strips 8½" × width of fabric.
  Subcut 3 rectangles 8½" × 3½" (E).
  Subcut 1 rectangle 8½" × 18" (F).
  Subcut 2 rectangles 8½" × 2½" (G).
  Subcut 1 rectangle 8½" × 6⅛" (H).
  Subcut 1 rectangle 8½" × 19" (J).
  Subcut 1 rectangle 8½" × 2⅜" (K).
  Subcut 1 rectangle 8½" × 8¼" (L).

- Cut 2 strips 4½" × width of fabric.
  Subcut 2 strips 4½" × 25½" (M).

- Cut 1 strip 1½" × width of fabric.
  Subcut 1 strip 1½" × 25½" (N).

- Cut 1 strip 3½" × width of fabric.
  Subcut 1 strip 3½" × 25½" (P).

- Cut 2 strips 9½" × width of fabric.
  Subcut 2 rectangles 9½" × 25½" (Q).

- Cut 1 strip 2½" × width of fabric.
  Subcut 1 strip 2½" × 25½" (R).

- From scraps, cut 2 squares 3½" × 3½" (X) and set aside for Put It Together, Step 5 (page 74).

TALK BUBBLE 1: **I love you**

1. Sew piece F to the left side of **I**.

2. Sew a piece E to the right side of **I**.

3. Sew A strips to the left side of **o** and between **o**, **v**, and **e**. .

4. Sew piece B to the top of **ove**.

5. Sew **l** to the left side of **ove**.

6. Sew piece H to the left side of **love** and piece E to the right side of **love**.

7. Sew A strips to the left side of **o** and between **o** and **u**.

8. Sew piece C to the bottom of **ou**.

9. Sew **y** to the left side of **ou**.

10. Sew piece L to the left side of **you** and a piece E to the right side of **you**.

11. Sew strip N between **I** and **love**.

12. Sew strip P between **love** and **you**.

13. Sew a strip M to the top of **I** and another to the bottom of **you**.

TALK BUBBLE 2: **I know**

1. Sew a piece G to the left side of **I** and sew piece J to the right side of **I**.

2. Sew A strips to the left side of **n** and between **n**, **o**, and **w**.

3. Sew piece D to the top of **now**.

4. Sew **k** to **now**.

5. Sew a piece G to the left side of **know** and sew piece K to the right side of **know**.

6. Sew strip R between **I** and **know**.

7. Sew a piece Q to the top of **I** and another to the bottom of **know**.

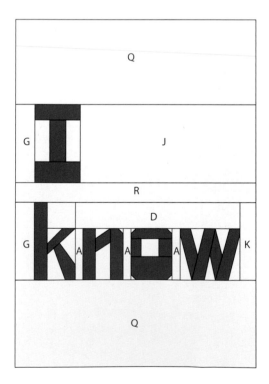

Put It Together

1. From the medium blue background fabric:

- Cut 1 piece 60½″ × width of fabric.

  Parallel to the selvage, subcut 1 strip 9½″ × 60½″ (A).

  Parallel to the selvage, subcut 1 strip 2½″ × 60½″ (H).

  Parallel to the selvage, subcut 1 strip 11½″ × 60½″.

  Subcut 1 strip 11½″ × 31½″ (C).
  Subcut 1 strip 11½″ × 4½″ (B).
  Subcut 1 strip 11½″ × 4½″, and then trim to 10½″ × 4½″ (F).
  Subcut 1 strip 11½″ × 2½″, and then trim to 10½″ × 2½″ (T).

  Parallel to the selvage, subcut 2 strips 4½″ × 60½″.

  Subcut 2 strips 4½″ × 31½″ (D).
  Subcut 1 strip 4½″ × 14½″ (E).
  Subcut 1 strip 4½″ × 4½″ (G).

- From scraps, cut 4 squares 2½″ × 2½″ (V).

2. From the dark blue background fabric:

- Cut 1 strip 60½″ × width of fabric.

    Parallel to the selvage, subcut 1 strip 9½″ × 60½″ (J).

    Parallel to the selvage, subcut 1 strip 2½″ × 60½″ (S).

    Parallel to the selvage, subcut 1 strip 11½″ × 60½″.

      Subcut 1 strip 11½″ × 31½″ (K).
      Subcut 1 strip 11½″ × 25½″, and then cut lengthwise into 1 strip 3½″ × 25½″ (M) and 1 strip 7½″ × 25½″ (N).

    Parallel to the selvage, subcut 2 strips 4½″ × 60½″.

      Subcut 1 strip 4½″ × 11½″ (L).
      Subcut 1 strip 4½″ × 31½″ (R).
      Subcut 2 strips 4½″ × 14½″ (P).
      Subcut 1 square 4½″ × 4½″ (Q).
      Subcut 1 strip 4½″ × 14½″, and then trim to 2½″ × 14½″ (U).

- From scraps, cut 2 squares 2½″ × 2½″ (W).

Detail of *Leia <3s Han*

3. Place a medium blue V square on the upper left and right corners of both talk bubbles to make snowball corners (page 135).

4. Place a dark blue W square on the bottom right corner of talk bubble 1 and the bottom left corner of talk bubble 2 to make snowball corners.

5. Create the points of the talk bubbles by placing X squares from the letter background fabric on the upper left corner of piece N and the upper right corner of piece M. Make a snowball corner on each.

6. Sew piece N to the bottom of talk bubble 1 (TB1).

7. Sew piece M to the bottom of talk bubble 2 (TB2).

8. Sew pieces B, Q, E, and P together.

9. Sew piece BQEP to the left side of TB1.

10. Sew pieces F, P, G, and L together.

11. Sew piece FPGL to the right side of TB2.

12. Sew piece T to the top of piece U.

13. Sew piece TU to the lower right side of TB1, leaving 4″ unsewn at the top end of the seam.

14. Sew a piece D to the top of piece K.

15. Sew piece DK to the bottom of TB1.

16. Sew TB2 to the TB1 unit next to pieces TU and DK. (Don't leave the seam open.)

17. Sew pieces C, R, and D together.

18. Sew piece CRD to the top of TB2.

19. Complete the open seam on piece TU, attaching piece CRD to the right side of TB1.

20. Sew strip S to the top of the talk bubbles and sew strip H to the bottom.

21. Sew strip A to the top of the talk bubbles and sew strip J to the bottom.

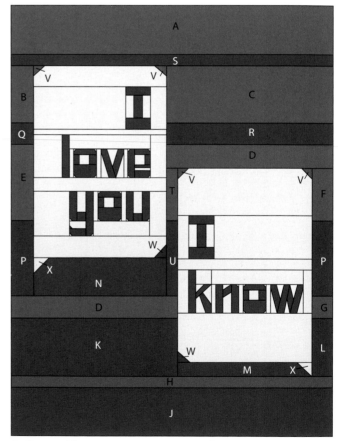

Quilt assembly

Leia <3s Han, 60½" × 80½"

Messages.
Shopping lists.
Appointments.
Words of wisdom.
Mash notes.
Compliments.
Leave them all here!

Talk to Me!

Finished wallhanging: 15½″ × 46¾″ Designed, pieced, and quilted by Sam Hunter, 2013

GO SHOPPING!

- **Talk bubbles:**
  ½ yard blackboard or
  chalkboard fabric

- **Letters:** ¼ yard black

- **Letter background:**
  ¼ yard orange

- **Border:** ½ yard
  turquoise print

- **Binding:** ⅜ yard orange

- **Backing:** 1⅓ yards

- **Batting:** 24″ × 55″

This quilt features fabrics from the Atomic collection by Michael Miller Fabrics and Kona Cotton Solids by Robert Kaufman Fabrics.

tip *Be careful not to touch your iron to the blackboard fabric or you will have a melting mess and a sticky iron. Iron through a cloth whenever possible, but still avoid getting heat near the blackboard fabric. I recommend finger-pressing all the seams that include the blackboard fabric.*

Print the Patterns

For the patterns, refer to the pullout. To adjust the printing, if necessary, refer to Reducing and Enlarging Patterns (page 13).

1. Print the following patterns at 80% (the uppercase **A** is 3″ tall):
  - Uppercase: **T, A, L, K**

2. Print the following patterns at 54% (the uppercase **O** is 2″ tall):
  - Uppercase: **T, O, M, E, !**

Make the Letters

For sewing techniques, refer to How to Paper Piece (page 10).

1. Cut 1 strip × width of fabric for each strip size to start. Cut more as needed.
  - Letters: 1¾″
  - Background: 2″

2. Paper piece the letters.

3. Press, trim, and remove the paper.

Make the Words

1. From letter background fabric:

- Cut 1 strip 3½″ × width of fabric.
  Subcut 3 rectangles 3½″ × ¾″ (A).
  Subcut 2 rectangles 3½″ × 1⅜″ (B).
  Trim the remainder of the strip
    to 2½″ wide.
  Subcut 2 rectangles 2½″ × ⅞″ (C).
  Subcut 1 rectangle 2½″ × 1⅜″ (D).
  Subcut 1 rectangle 2½″ × 1″ (E).
  Subcut 2 rectangles 2½″ × 1⅝″ (F).

- Cut 1 strip 1¼″ × width of fabric.
  Subcut 3 rectangles 1¼″ × 12½″ (G).

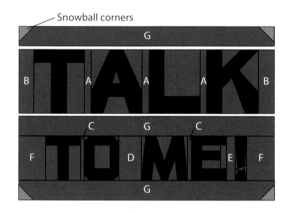

Snowball corners

2. Sew A strips between **T**, **A**, **L**, and **K**.

3. Sew a B strip to each end of **TALK**.

4. Sew a C strip between **T** and **O**.

5. Sew a C strip between **M** and **E**.

6. Sew piece D between **TO** and **ME**.

7. Sew strip E between **ME** and **!**.

8. Sew a piece F to each end of **TO ME!**

9. Sew a G strip between **TALK** and **TO ME!**

10. Sew G strips above **TALK** and below **TO ME!** The snowball corners will be added later.

Make the Talk Bubbles

1. From blackboard fabric:
- Cut 3 rectangles 9½″ × 12½″.
- Cut 3 squares 2½″ × 2½″.

2. From border fabric:
- Cut 1 strip 3½″ × width of fabric.
  Subcut 3 rectangles 3½″ × 12½″.

- Cut 1 strip 1½″ × width of fabric.
  Subcut 9 squares 1½″ × 1½″.
  Subcut and trim 4 squares 1″ × 1″.

3. To make the talk bubble points, place a 2½″ square of blackboard fabric on each of the 3 border rectangles to make snowball corners (page 135). Refer to the construction diagram (next page) to make 2 corners on the left and 1 on the right. Be sure the points face the right way!

4. To make the talk bubble corners, place 1½″ squares of border fabric on 3 corners of each talk bubble to make snowball corners. Note that 2 bubbles point to the left and 1 to the right, so be sure to get the squares in the correct corners. For these corners, do not trim the excess fabric from the back of the triangle; leave it in place to give extra structure to the corners.

5. Sew the bubbles and rectangles together.

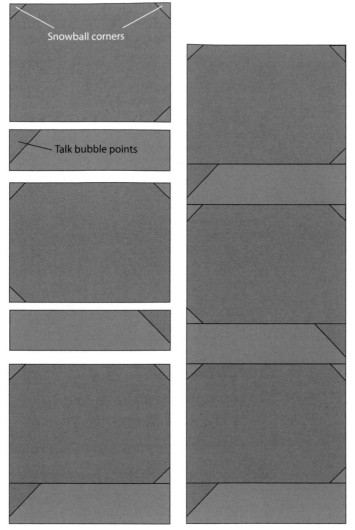

Talk bubble construction

6. Place the 1″ squares of border fabric on the 4 corners of the word block to make 4 snowball corners.

Add the Outer Border

1. From border fabric:

- Cut 4 strips 2″ × width of fabric.

- Sew the strips together end to end along the short edges, using straight or diagonal seams. Use the method that works best for the print you are using. Refer to Diagonal Seams (page 135).
  Subcut 2 strips 2″ × 12½″.
  Subcut 2 strips 2″ × 46¾″.

2. Sew 2″ × 12½″ strips to the top and bottom of the word block.

3. Sew the word block to the top of the talk bubbles.

4. Sew a 2″ × 46¾″ strip to the left side of the talk bubbles and word block unit.

5. Add the pocket for chalk (page 80) before adding the border to the right side.

ADD THE POCKET

1. From border fabric:
- Cut 1 rectangle 3½˝ × 8˝.

2. Fold the rectangle in half with wrong sides together to make a pocket that is 3½˝ along the fold and 4˝ deep. Press.

3. Place the pocket on the lower right corner of the third talk bubble and baste a scant ¼˝ from the edge.

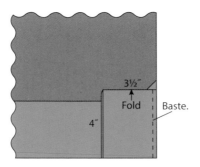

4. Sew the remaining 2˝ × 46¾˝ border strip to the right side of the talk bubbles, sewing the left edge of the pocket into the seam. Press the pocket outward across the border. Yes, the pocket is larger than the space!

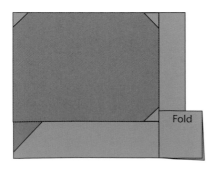

5. Baste the right side of the pocket to the outer edge of the border a scant ¼˝ from the edge. Make a pleat at each edge along the bottom of the pocket, press, and baste along the bottom a scant ¼˝ from the edge.

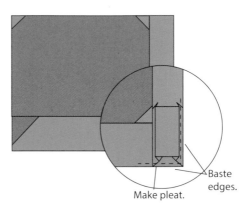

Finish the Wallhanging

1. Layer, baste, and quilt as desired. When quilting the outer border, be sure not to quilt over the pocket!

2. Add the binding to the quilt, covering the basting stitches along the bottom and right side of the pocket.

Detail of *Talk to Me!*

Talk to Me!, 15½" × 46¾"

Wacky Races and other Hanna-Barbera cartoons were a Saturday morning staple of my childhood. Bumbling villain Dick Dastardly is foiled yet again. His trusty, snarky sidekick, Muttley, wheezes out a laugh, mumbling something under his breath. What was that? Part growl? Part muttering? Part something that might not be PG? Never mind; we have symbols for that!

Rackafrax!

Finished quilt: 50½″ × 72¼″

Designed, pieced, and quilted by Sam Hunter, 2013

☀ GO SHOPPING!

- **Color bands:** 25 assorted print strips 2½″ × width of fabric, or 1 precut strip pack

- **Characters:** ⅛ yard each of 9 coordinating prints *or* use remaining precut strips*

- **Body background:** 2 yards cream print

- **Character background and sashing strip:** 1½ yards orange

- **Binding:** ⅝ yard orange *or* use remaining precut strips to make scrappy binding

- **Backing:** 3½ yards

- **Batting:** 59″ × 80″

This quilt features fabrics from the Comma collection by Brigitte Heitland of Zen Chic for Moda Fabrics and Kona Solids by Robert Kaufman Fabrics.

* For the @ character, you'll need 2 strips of the same fabric or ⅛ yard purchased separately.

Print the Patterns

For the patterns, refer to the pullout and Patterns (pages 136–138, 140, and 141). To adjust the printing, if necessary, refer to Reducing and Enlarging Patterns (page 13).

Print the following patterns at 200% (the @ is 7½″ tall):

- Punctuation: **@** (at sign), ***** (asterisk), **** (backslash), **$** (dollar sign), **+** (plus), **(** (left parenthesis), **#** (hash), **%** (percent), **!** (exclamation point)

- Angled Exclamation Point Surround pattern

Make the Characters

For sewing techniques, refer to How to Paper Piece (page 10). If you are working with a jelly roll or bundle of precut strips, you may want to choose the 25 strips to use in the body of the quilt before piecing the characters. See Make the Strip Set, Step 2 (page 85).

1. Cut 1 strip × width of fabric for each strip size to start. Cut more as needed.

   - Characters: 2½″ if using a precut strip pack. If using yardage, start with a 2¾″ strip. For the @ (at sign), use 2 precut strips of similar color and value, or cut both strips from a larger cut of coordinating fabric.

   - Background: 2½″, 3″, 3½″, 4″

Consider using a single name or the name of a sports team (**Go Team!**) to make this quilt your own.

When designing words or a phrase to fit this project, give the words a couple of inches of breathing room.

The word block is 50″ × 10″ finished, so design your words to be no wider than 46″. Or, you could add more lines of text and lengthen the quilt accordingly.

To design and print your words at the correct size, refer to Designing Custom Text (page 30) and Reducing and Enlarging Patterns (page 13).

2. Paper piece the characters. In some places, the 2½″ strips are a tight fit. Be sure to pin the pieces to test them before sewing.

   Set the **!** (exclamation point) into the Angled Exclamation Point Surround, following the instructions on the surround pattern (page 138).

3. Press, trim, and remove the paper.

Make the "Word"

1. From character background fabric:
   - Cut 1 strip 8″ × width of fabric.
     Subcut 8 rectangles 8″ × 1¼″ (A).
     Subcut 2 rectangles 8″ × 3⅛″ (B).

   - Cut 4 strips 1¾″ × width of fabric.
     Sew end to end along the short edges using diagonal seams. Refer to Diagonal Seams (page 135).
     Subcut 3 strips 1¾″ × 50½″ (C). Use 2 strips for Step 4. Set aside 1 strip for putting the top together.

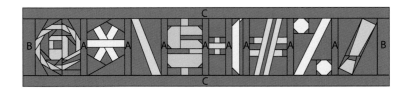

2. Sew A strips between the characters, but not to the left side of @ or the right side of **!**.

3. Sew a B strip to the left side of @ and another to the right side of **!**. Trim if necessary to measure 50½″ long.

4. Sew C strips to the top and bottom of @*\$+(#%**!**.

Make the Strip Set

1. From background fabric:

- Cut 25 strips 2½″ × width of fabric.

2. From precut strips:

- Choose 25 main strips that contrast well with the body background.

3. Line up the main strips vertically on a design surface, moving the colors and patterns around until you like the result. Use sticky notes or blue painter's tape to number the vertical rows in order from 1 to 25.

4. Refer to the chart to trim the background strips and the main strips to the correct lengths.

Row	Main strip	Background strip
1	27″	36″
2	31″	32″
3	25″	38″
4	35″	28″
5	21″	42″
6	37″	26″
7	27″	36″
8	33″	30″
9	25″	38″
10	22″	41″
11	29″	34″
12	34″	29″
13	35″	28″
14	27″	36″
15	28″	35″
16	25″	38″
17	30″	33″
18	37″	26″
19	28″	35″
20	36″	27″
21	24″	39″
22	39″	24″
23	33″	30″
24	25″	38″
25	30″	33″

5. Pair each background strip with its corresponding main strip and sew together. Sew the paired strips together into 1 unit.

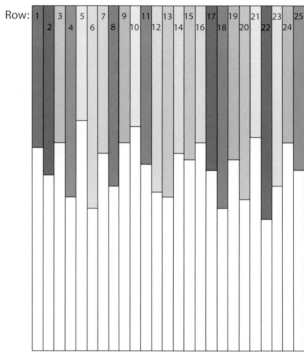

Strip set assembly

> **tip** To avoid distortion when sewing long strips together, pin them first at the ends and middle.
>
> When sewing lots of strips together, sew them in pairs first and press; then sew the pairs together. Press well, being careful not to stretch the strips as you press.

6. From the top of the strip set:

- Cut a 5½″ segment across the width.
- Cut a 10½″ segment across the width.

You will have approximately 46″ remaining. Trim to 46″, or keep any extra length if you want your quilt to be a bit longer.

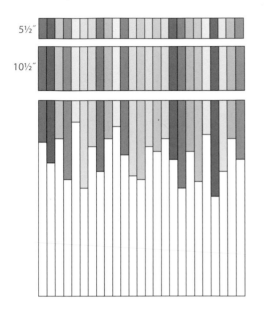

5½″

10½″

Put It Together

1. Sew the word block to the bottom of the 10½″ strip set segment.

2. Sew the 46″ segment to the bottom of the word block.

3. Sew the remaining C strip to the bottom of the 46″ segment.

4. Sew the 5½″ segment to the bottom of strip C.

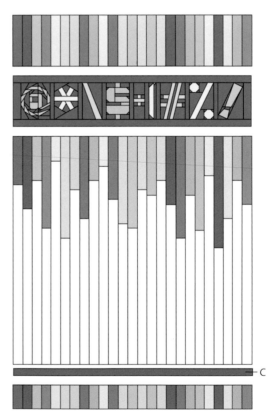

—C

Quilt assembly

Detail of *Rackafrax!*

Rackafrax!, 50½˝ × 72¼˝

A simple statement or a complex journey? Do what you love or love what you do? Either way, when you get there, it's a good thing. If you aren't doing what you love, try to find a way to love what you do while you find a way to get to where you will love to be.

Love What You Do

Finished wallhanging: 17½″ × 37½″ Designed, pieced, and quilted by Sam Hunter, 2013

✳ GO SHOPPING!

- **Background:** 1¼ yards dark blue

- **Letters for LOVE and WHAT:** ⅛ yard each of 2 different colors

- **Letters for YOU and DO:** ¼ yard each of 2 different colors

- **Heart:** ⅛ yard for outside and ⅛ yard for inside (or scraps from letters)

- **Optional interfacing:*** 2¼ yards Pellon 906F Fusible Sheerweight interfacing

- **Binding:** ⅜ yard

- **Backing:** 1⅓ yards

- **Batting:** 26″ × 46″

* Use with Radiance cotton/silk blend or other silky, shiny, or delicate fabric.

This quilt features fabrics from the Radiance collection, a cotton/silk blend by Robert Kaufman Fabrics, and the Quilter's Shadow collection by Stof.dk.

Print the Patterns

For the patterns, refer to the pullout. To adjust the printing, if necessary, refer to Reducing and Enlarging Patterns (page 13).

1. Print **LOVE** in uppercase at 107% (the uppercase **L** is 4″ tall).

2. Print the heart at 240% (the heart is 9″ tall).

3. Print **WHAT** in uppercase at 100% (the uppercase **W** is 3¾″ tall).

4. Print **YOU** in uppercase at 146% (the uppercase **Y** is 5½″ tall).

5. Print **DO** in uppercase at 220% (the uppercase **D** is 8¼″ tall).

Make the Letters

For sewing techniques, refer to How to Paper Piece (page 10).

1. If you are using a cotton/silk blend poplin or other delicate fabric, fuse the interfacing to the wrong side of the fabric before cutting, following the manufacturer's instructions.

2. Cut 1 strip × width of fabric for each strip size to start. Cut more as needed.

- Letters for **DO**: 3¼″
- Letters for **WHAT**: 2¼″
- Letters for **YOU**: 2¾″
- Letters for **LOVE**: 2″
- Heart outline: 2½″
- Heart center: 4″
- Background: 4″

3. Paper piece the largest letters first. Use the background scraps from the larger letters to sew the smaller letters.

4. Press, trim, and remove the paper.

Make the Words

1. From background fabric:

   ■ Cut 1 strip 9½″ × width of fabric.
     Subcut 2 rectangles 9½″ × 4⅛″ (A).
     Subcut and trim 1 rectangle 1¾″ × 8¾″ (B).
     Subcut and trim 2 rectangles 1³⁄₁₆″ × 6″ (C).*
     Subcut and trim 3 rectangles 1⅛″ × 4½″ (D).
     Subcut and trim 3 rectangles 1″ × 4¼″ (E).

   *Note: ³⁄₁₆″ is halfway between ⅛″ and ¼″ on your ruler.

2. Sew an A piece to each side of the heart.

3. Sew strip B between **D** and **O**.

4. Sew C strips between **Y**, **O**, and **U**.

5. Sew D strips between **L**, **O**, **V**, and **E**.

6. Sew E strips between **W**, **H**, **A**, and **T**.

Put It Together

1. From background fabric:

   ■ Cut 4 strips 1¾″ × width of fabric.
     Subcut 4 rectangles 1¾″ × 15″ (F).
     Subcut 2 strips 1¾″ × 37½″ (H).

   ■ Cut 1 strip 1¼″ × width of fabric.
     Subcut 2 rectangles 1¼″ × 15″ (G).

2. Sew G strips to the top and bottom of the heart.

3. Sew F strips to the top of **LOVE** and **YOU** and to the top and bottom of **DO**.

4. Sew **LOVE** to the top of the heart.

5. Sew **WHAT** to the bottom of the heart.

6. Sew **YOU** to the bottom of **WHAT**.

7. Sew **DO** to the bottom of **YOU**.

8. Sew an H strip to each side of the word blocks to complete the quilt top.

Quilt assembly

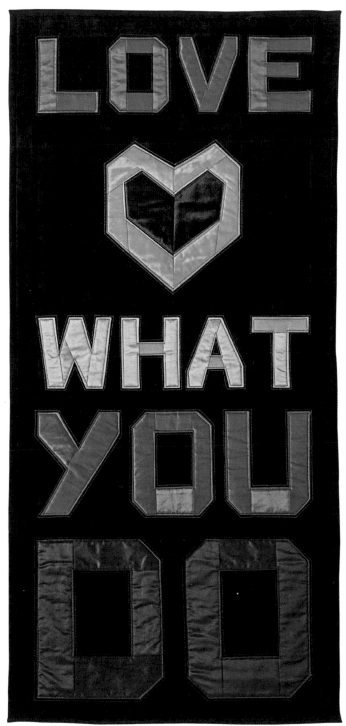

Love What You Do, 17½″ × 37½″

She used to just be normal. She used to be just plain-vanilla-ice-cream nice. And then it happened … she touched the fabric. And that was that! You've met her. You're friends with her. You might even be her. … While all my beloved quilt pals really are nice, there's another wilder, authentic side to us that quilting brings forth. And it's a whole lot more fun than just being nice.

She Was a Nice Girl...

Finished lap quilt: 44½" × 62¾" Designed, pieced, and quilted by Sam Hunter, 2013

 GO SHOPPING!

- **Background:**
  3¾ yards light gray

- **Letters for nice:**
  ¼ yard pink floral or print that characterizes the word **nice**

- **Letters for quilting:**
  ⅛ yard each *or* scraps of 8 assorted zany prints that characterize the word **quilting**

- **Letters for all other words:** 1 yard dark gray

- **Binding:** ⅝ yard print

- **Backing:** 3 yards

- **Batting:** 53" × 71"

This quilt features fabrics from the Painter's Canvas collection by Laura Gunn for Michael Miller Fabrics, fabrics from the Sketch Basic collection by Timeless Treasures, and various other fabrics from my stash.

Print the Patterns

For the patterns, refer to the pullout. To adjust the printing, if necessary, refer to Reducing and Enlarging Patterns (page 13).

1. Print **she was a** in lowercase at 160% (the lowercase **e** is 4" tall).

2. Print **nice** in lowercase at 240% (the lowercase **n** is 6" tall).

3. Print **girl** in lowercase at 140% (the lowercase **r** is 3½" tall).

4. Print **until** in lowercase at 110% (the lowercase **u** is 2¾" tall).

5. Print **she** in lowercase at 180% (the lowercase **e** is 4½" tall).

6. Print **took up** in lowercase at 170% (the lowercase **o** is 4¼" tall).

7. Print **quilting** in lowercase at 220% (the lowercase **u** is 5½" tall).

Make the Letters

For sewing techniques, refer to How to Paper Piece (page 10).

1. Cut 1 strip × width of fabric for each strip size to start. Cut more as needed.
  - Letters for **she was a**, **girl**, and **until**: 2"
  - Letters for **she took up**: 2¼", 2½", 3"
  - Letters for **nice**: 2½"
  - Letters for **quilting**: 2½", 3"
  - Background: 2", 2½", 3", 3½", 4"

2. Paper piece the letters.

3. Press, trim, and remove the paper.

Make the Words

For this project, all measurements are rounded up to the nearest ⅛″ to save the headache of trying to measure ⅟₁₆″ or ⅟₃₂″. This means that you might occasionally have a strip that is a couple of threads too big. Sew the strips onto the letters and trim as needed.

 tip *The instructions for setting each word or phrase begin with cutting new strips. Always check your leftover pieces before cutting to save fabric!*

she was a

1. From background fabric:
   - Cut 1 strip 1⅛″ × width of fabric.
     Subcut 4 rectangles 1⅛″ × 4½″ (A).
   - Cut 1 strip 3¼″ × width of fabric.
     Subcut 2 rectangles 3¼″ × 4½″ (B).
     Subcut and trim 1 rectangle 2½″ × 4⅜″ (C).
     Subcut and trim 1 strip 2½″ × 25⅜″ (D).

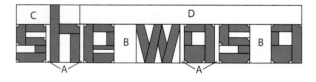

2. Sew an A strip to the right side of the first **s**.

3. Sew an A strip to the left side of **e**.

4. Sew an A strip to each side of the first **a**.

5. Sew piece C to the top of the first **s**.

6. Sew the first **s** to **h**.

7. Sew the first **a** between **w** and the second **s** to make **was**.

8. Sew a B piece between **e** and **w**.

9. Sew a B piece between **was** and **a**.

10. Sew strip D to the top of **e was a**.

11. Sew **sh** to **e was a**.

nice

1. From background fabric:
   - Cut 1 strip 3½″ × width of fabric.
     Subcut 1 rectangle 3½″ × 6⅛″ (E).
     Subcut 1 rectangle 3½″ × 11⅞″ (F).
     Subcut and trim 3 rectangles 1⅜″ × 6½″ (G).

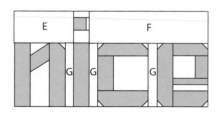

2. Sew a G strip to the right side of **n**.

3. Sew a G strip to the left side of **c**.

4. Sew a G strip between **c** and **e**.

5. Sew piece E to the top of **n**.

6. Sew piece F to the top of **ce**.

7. Sew **i** between **n** and **ce**.

girl

1. From background fabric:

- Cut 1 strip 2¼″ × width of fabric.
  Subcut 2 rectangles 2¼″ × 3⅜″ (H).
  Subcut 1 rectangle 2¼″ × 6⅝″ (J).
  Subcut and trim 3 rectangles
  1″ × 5¾″ (K).

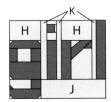

2. Sew an H piece to the top of **g**.
Trim as needed.

3. Sew an H piece to the top of **r**.
Trim as needed.

4. Sew K strips to the left side of **i** and
between **i**, **r**, and **l**.

5. Sew piece J to the bottom of **irl**.
Trim as needed.

6. Sew **g** to **irl**.

until

1. From background fabric:

- Cut 1 strip 1⅞″ × width of fabric.
  Subcut 1 rectangle 1⅞″ × 5¾″ (L).
  Subcut and trim 2 rectangles
  ⅞″ × 3¼″ (M).
  Subcut and trim 2 rectangles
  ⅞″ × 4⅝″ (N).

2. Sew an M strip to each side of **n**.

3. Sew **u** to **n**.

4. Sew piece L to the top of **un**.
Trim as needed.

5. Sew an N strip to each side of **i**.

6. Sew **i** between **t** and **l**.

7. Sew **un** to **til**.

Detail of *She Was
a Nice Girl…*

she

1. From background fabric:
   - Cut 1 strip 2¾″ × width of fabric.
     Subcut 2 rectangles 2¾″ × 4⅞″ (P).
     Subcut and trim 2 rectangles
     1¼″ × 5″ (Q).

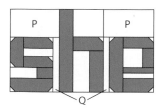

2. Sew Q strips to the right side of **s** and the left side of **e**.

3. Sew a piece P to the top of **s** and another to the top of **e**.

4. Sew **h** between **s** and **e**.

took up

1. From background fabric:
   - Cut 1 strip 3½″ × width of fabric.
     Subcut 1 rectangle 3½″ × 6⅞″ (R).
     Subcut and trim 4 rectangles
     1⅛″ × 4¾″ (S).

   - Cut 1 strip 2⅝″ × width of fabric.
     Subcut 1 rectangle 2⅝″ × 4½″ (T).
     Subcut 1 rectangle 2⅝″ × 3⅞″ (U).
     Subcut 1 rectangle 2⅝″ × 9⅛″ (V).
     Subcut 1 rectangle 2⅝″ × 22½″ (W).

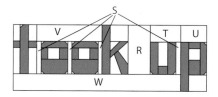

2. Sew an S strip between the 2 **o** letters.

3. Sew an S strip to each side of **oo** and to the right side of **u**.

4. Sew piece V to the top of **oo**.
   Trim as needed.

5. Sew piece R to the right side of **k**.

6. Sew piece T to the top of **u**.
   Trim as needed.

7. Sew piece U to the top of **p**.

8. Sew **t** to **oo**.

9. Sew **too** to **k**.

10. Sew **took** to **u**.

11. Sew piece W to the bottom of **took u**.

12. Sew **took u** to **p**.

quilting

1. From background fabric:
   - Cut 2 strips 3¼″ × width of fabric.
     Subcut 2 rectangles 3¼″ × 5″ (X).
     Subcut 1 strip 3¼″ × 23½″ (Y).
     Subcut 2 rectangles 3¼″ × 6¾″ (Z).
     Subcut and trim 4 rectangles
         1⅜″ × 6″ (AA).

   - Cut 1 strip 1⅜″ × width of fabric.
     Subcut 3 rectangles 1⅜″ × 8¾″ (BB).

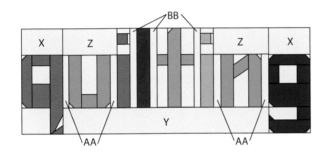

2. Sew a piece X to the top of **q** and another
   to the top of **g**. Trim as needed.

3. Sew an AA strip to each side of **u** and to
   each side of **n**.

4. Sew a piece Z to the top of **u** and another
   to the top of **n**. Trim as needed.

5. Sew BB strips between **i**, **l**, **t**, and **i**.

6. Sew **u** to **ilti**.

7. Sew **uilti** to **n**.

8. Sew strip Y to the bottom of **uiltin**.
   Trim as needed.

9. Sew **q** to **uiltin** and **quiltin** to **g**.

Put It Together

1. From background fabric:
   - Cut 1 strip 11½″ × width of fabric.
     Subcut 1 rectangle 11½″ × 9″ (A).
     Subcut 1 rectangle 11½″ × 4½″ (B).
     Trim the remaining strip to 9½″ wide.
     Subcut 1 rectangle 9½″ × 4½″ (C).
     Subcut 1 rectangle 9½″ × 22¼″ (D).

   - Cut 1 strip 9″ × width of fabric.
     Subcut 1 rectangle 9″ × 15⅛″ (E).
     Subcut 1 rectangle 9″ × 4½″ (F).
     Trim the remaining strip to 6½″.
     Subcut 1 rectangle 6½″ × 4½″ (G).
     Subcut 1 rectangle 6½″ × 8¾″ (H).

   - Cut 1 strip 7¼″ × width of fabric.
     Subcut 1 rectangle 7¼″ × 28¼″ (J).
     Subcut 1 rectangle 7¼″ × 4½″ (K).

   - Cut 1 strip 7½″ × width of fabric.
     Subcut 1 rectangle 7½″ × 9¾″, and
         then trim to 3⅜″ × 9¾″ (L).
     Subcut 1 rectangle 7½″ × 18½″ (M).
     Subcut 2 rectangles 7½″ × 4½″ (N).

   - Cut 3 strips 4½″ × width of fabric.
     Sew together end to end with
     diagonal seams. Refer to Diagonal
     Seams (page 135).
     Subcut 2 strips 4½″ × 44½″ (P).

   - Cut 3 strips 2″ × width of fabric.
     Sew together end to end.
     Subcut 2 strips 2″ × 44½″ (Q).

   - Cut 4 strips 1½″ × width of fabric.
     Sew together end to end.
     Subcut 3 strips 1½″ × 44½″ (R).

2. Sew piece A to the left side of **quilting**.

3. Sew piece B to right side of **quilting**. Trim the A side if needed so the row measures 44½″ long.

4. Sew piece C to the left side of **nice**.

5. Sew piece D to the right side of **nice**. Trim the D side if needed so the row measures 44½″ long.

6. Sew piece E to the left side of **took up**.

7. Sew piece F to the right side of **took up**. Trim the E side if needed so the row measures 44½″ long.

8. Sew piece G to the left side of **she was a**.

9. Sew piece H to the right side of **she was a**. Trim the H side if needed so the row measures 44½″ long.

10. Sew piece J to the left side of **she**.

11. Sew piece K to the right side of **she**.

12. Sew piece L to the top of **until**. Trim as needed.

13. Sew piece M between **girl** and **until**.

14. Sew an N piece to each side of **girl until**.

15. Sew a P strip to the top of **she was a** and another to the bottom of **quilting**.

16. Sew a Q strip to the bottom of **nice** and **girl until**.

17. Sew R strips to the bottom of **she was a**, **she**, and **took up**.

18. Sew the rows together to complete the quilt top.

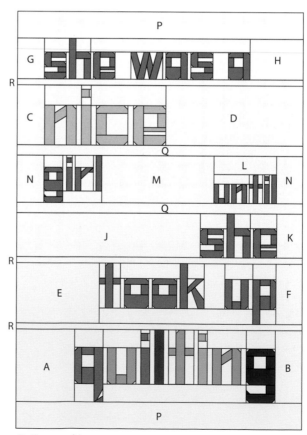

Quilt assembly

She Was a Nice Girl…, 44½″ × 62¾″

she just IGNORED the people who said it couldn't be DONE

Some people cheer you onward and upward. Others are naysayers, people who would hamper your flights of fancy and ambition with their small-thinking words. Best to just ignore those people, yes?

She Just Ignored People

Finished lap quilt: 51" × 70¾"

Designed, pieced, and quilted by Sam Hunter, 2013

✳ GO SHOPPING!

- **Letter background:**
  2½ yards purple

- **Main letters:**
  1 yard cream

- **Accent letters
  (IGNORED, DONE):**
  ⅜ yard lime green

- **Inner border:**
  ¼ yard purple stripe

- **Outer border:**
  1½ yards print*

- **Binding:** ⅝ yard purple

- **Backing:** 3⅓ yards

- **Batting:** 59" × 79"

This quilt features fabrics from the Collage collection by Carrie Bloomston of SUCH Designs for Windham Fabrics.

* *I used a border print.*

Print the Patterns

For the letter patterns, refer to the pullout. For the apostrophe, refer to the apostrophe pattern (page 141). To adjust the printing, if necessary, refer to Reducing and Enlarging Patterns (page 13).

Print the following patterns at 100% (the lowercase **e** is 2½" tall; the uppercase **I** is 3¾" tall).

- Uppercase: **D** (2), **E** (2), **I**, **G**, **N** (2), **O** (2), **R**

- Lowercase: **a**, **b**, **c**, **d** (2), **e** (5), **h** (3), **i** (2), **j**, **l** (2), **n**, **o** (3), **p** (2), **s** (3), **t** (4), **u** (2), **w**

- Punctuation: **'** (apostrophe)

Make the Letters

For sewing techniques, refer to How to Paper Piece (page 10).

1. Cut 1 strip × width of fabric for each strip size to start. Cut more as needed.
  - Letters: 2", 2½"
  - Background: 2", 2½"

2. Paper piece the letters; remember to use the accent fabric for the uppercase letters only.

3. Press, trim, and remove the paper.

When designing a personalized phrase to fit this project, give the words a couple of inches of breathing room.

You can create 7 lines of text at 100% or make larger words (but fewer of them). The word block is 34½″ × 47¾″ finished, so design your words to be no larger than 30″ × 43″.

To design and print your words at the correct size, refer to Designing Custom Text (page 30) and Reducing and Enlarging Patterns (page 13).

QUILT STORY

I met Carrie Bloomston (who designed the fabric I used in this project) a couple of years ago at the Long Beach Quilt Festival. We immediately connected when we discovered that we were both graduates of and refugees from challenging art programs. We talked a lot about what it took to regain our own authentic artistic voices after such an experience. I designed this quilt for both of us, as a reminder to never lose our voices again.

Make the Words

You will cut the setting pieces for all the words at the same time. Mark the pieces with sticky notes or blue painter's tape to keep them in order. If you have a design wall, place the parts on the wall with the words as you cut.

1. From letter background fabric:

- Cut 1 strip 4¼″ × width of fabric.
  Subcut 15 rectangles 4¼″ × ⅞″ (A).
  Subcut 4 rectangles 4¼″ × 2″ (B).
  Trim the remaining strip to 3″ wide.
  Subcut 20 rectangles 3″ × ⅞″ (C).

- Cut 3 strips 1¾″ × width of fabric.
  Subcut 6 rectangles 1¾″ × 2⅞″ (D).
  Subcut 1 rectangle 1¾″ × 8¾″ (E).
  Subcut 2 rectangles 1¾″ × 5⅝″ (F).
  Subcut 1 rectangle 1¾″ × 7⅜″ (G).
  Subcut 1 rectangle 1¾″ × 8½″ (H).
  Subcut 1 rectangle 1¾″ × 9⅝″ (J).
  Subcut 1 rectangle 1¾″ × 3⅞″ (K).
  Subcut 1 rectangle 1¾″ × 3¾″ (L).
  Subcut 1 rectangle 1¾″ × 5¼″ (M).
  Subcut 1 rectangle 1¾″ × 7⅝″ (N).
  Subcut 1 rectangle 1¾″ × 3¼″ (P).

she just

1. Sew C strips to the right side of **s** and the left side of **e**.

2. Sew D pieces to the top of **s** and the top of **e**.

3. Sew **s** to **h**.

4. Sew **sh** to **e**.

5. Sew a B piece to the right side of **she**.

6. Sew piece E to the bottom of **she**.

7. Sew a C strip to each side of **u** and to the right side of **s**.

8. Sew **u** to **s**.

9. Sew an F piece to the top of **us**.

10. Sew **t** to the right side of **us**.

11. Sew piece G to the bottom of **ust**.

12. Sew **j** to the left side of **ust**.

13. Sew **she** to **just**.

IGNORED

Sew A strips between the letters of **IGNORED**, but not to either end of the word.

the people

1. Sew an A strip between **t** and **h**.

2. Sew a C strip to the left side of **e**.

3. Sew a D piece to the top of **e**.

4. Sew **th** to this **e**.

5. Sew a piece B to the right side of **the**.

6. Sew piece H to the bottom of **the**.

7. Sew a C strip to each side of the second **e** and to the right side of **o**.

8. Sew **e** to this **o**.

9. Sew an F piece to the bottom of **eo**.

10. Sew a **p** to each end of **eo**.

11. Sew piece J to the top of **peop**.

12. Sew an A strip to the left side of **l**.

13. Sew a C strip to the left side of **e**.

14. Sew a D piece to the top of **e**.

15. Sew **l** to **e**.

16. Sew piece K to the bottom of **le**.

17. Sew **peop** to **le**.

18. Sew **the** to **people**.

who said it

1. Sew C strips to the right side of **w** and the left side of **o**.

2. Sew piece L to the top of **w**.

3. Sew a D piece to the top of **o**.

4. Sew **w** to **h**.

5. Sew **wh** to **o**.

6. Sew a B piece to the right side of **who**.

7. Sew C strips to the right side of **s** and the right side of **a**.

8. Sew **s** to **a**.

9. Sew piece M to the top of **sa**.

10. Sew an A strip between the first **i** and **d**.

11. Sew **sa** to **id**.

12. Sew a B piece to the right side of **said**.

13. Sew **who** to **said**.

14. Sew an A strip between **i** and **t**.

15. Sew **who said** to **it**.

couldn't

1. Sew C strips to the right side of **c**, the right side of **o**, and the right side of **u**.

2. Sew **c** to **o**.

3. Sew **co** to **u**.

4. Sew piece N to the top of **cou**.

5. Sew **l** to **cou**.

6. Sew an A strip to the right side of **l**.

7. Sew **coul** to **d**.

8. Sew C strips to each side of **n**.

9. Sew piece P to the top of **n**.

10. Sew **could** to **n**.

11. Sew the apostrophe to **couldn**.

12. Sew an A strip to the right side of the apostrophe.

13. Sew **couldn'** to **t**.

be

1. Sew a C strip to the left side of **e**.

2. Sew a D piece to the top of **e**.

3. Sew **b** to **e**.

DONE

Sew A strips between the letters of **DONE**, but not to either end of the word.

Put It Together

1. From letter background fabric:

- Cut 2 strips 4¾″ × width of fabric.
  Subcut 2 strips 4¾″ × 35″ (A).

- Cut 3 strips 2″ × width of fabric.
  Subcut 3 strips 2″ × 35″ (B).

- Cut 3 strips 2½″ × width of fabric.
  Subcut 3 strips 2½″ × 35″ (C).

- Cut 1 strip 5½″ × width of fabric.
  Subcut 2 rectangles 5½″ × 9½″ (D).
  Subcut 2 rectangles 5½″ × 7½″ (E).

- Cut 3 strips 4¼″ × width of fabric.
  Subcut 2 rectangles 4¼″ × 6⅝″ (F).
  Subcut 2 rectangles 4¼″ × 7¼″ (G).
  Subcut 2 rectangles 4¼″ × 10″ (H).
  Subcut 2 rectangles 4¼″ × 15⅝″ (J).
  Subcut 2 rectangles 4¼″ × 11¼″ (K).

2. Sew a D piece to each side of **she just**.

3. Sew an F piece to each side of **IGNORED**.

4. Sew an E piece to each side of **the people**.

5. Sew a G piece to each side of **who said it**.

6. Sew an H piece to each side of **couldn't**.

7. Sew a J piece to each side of **be**.

8. Sew a K piece to each side of **DONE**.

9. Sew an A strip to the top of **she just**.

10. Sew an A strip to the bottom of **DONE**.

11. Sew B strips between **she just**, **IGNORED**, **the people**, and **who said it**.

12. Sew C strips between **who said it**, **couldn't**, **be**, and **DONE**.

13. Measure the quilt center and trim equal amounts from the sides as needed so that it measures 35″ × 48¼″.

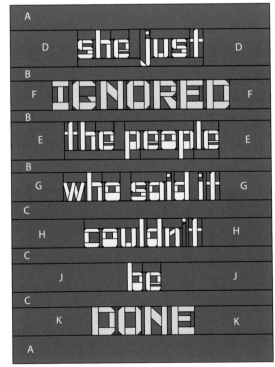

Quilt assembly

Add the Inner Border

1. From inner border fabric:

- Cut 5 strips 1″ × width of fabric. Sew together end to end using diagonal seams. Refer to Diagonal Seams (page 135).

  Subcut 2 strips 1″ × 48¼″.

  Subcut 2 strips 1″ × 36″.

2. Sew a 48¼″ strip to each side of the quilt top.

3. Sew 36″ strips to the top and bottom.

Add the Outer Border

1. From outer border fabric:

- Cut 3 strips *parallel* to the selvage 8″ × length of fabric. If you are using a border print, cut from the side opposite the border print.

  Subcut 2 strips 8″ × 49¼″ for the side borders.

  Subcut 1 strip 8″ × 51″ for the top border.

- If you are not using fabric with a border print, cut 1 more strip parallel to the selvage 8″ × length of fabric.

  Subcut 1 strip 8″ × 51″ for the bottom border.

If you are using fabric with a border print, see the tip below.

 tip — **Using a Border Print:** *Cut the bottom border strip from the border print, changing the width measurement as necessary to include the depth of the border design. I cut my bottom border 14½″ wide.*

2. Sew the side borders to the quilt top.

3. Sew the top and bottom borders to the quilt top.

Detail of *She Just Ignored People*

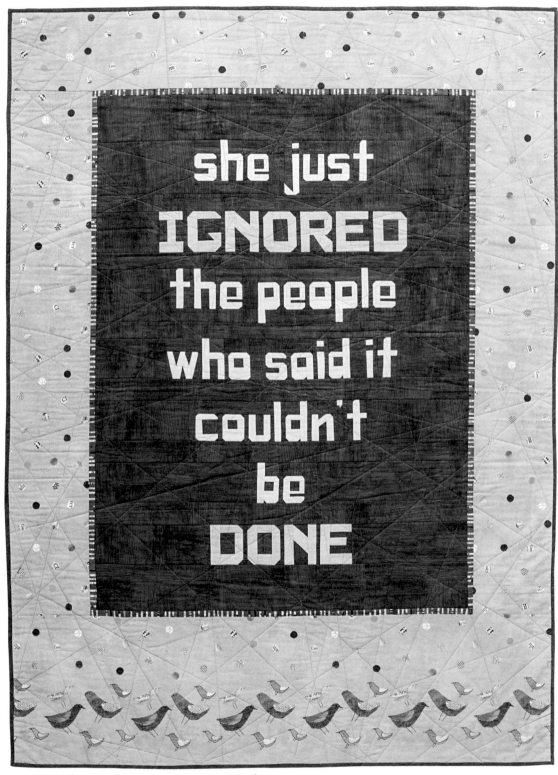

She Just Ignored People, 51˝ × 70¾˝

One of my favorite things in the world to do is to eat with friends. There's something special about the interchange of ideas and friendship over good food. From comfort food to gourmet recipes, any homemade goodness looks better on a pretty table. So come and get it! Bon appétit! Eat!

EAT

Finished place mats: 13″ × 19″ each   Designed, pieced, and quilted by Sam Hunter, 2013

 GO SHOPPING!

For each place mat

- Letters: ⅛ yard

- Letter background and border: ⅓ yard

- Center and backing: ½ yard (⅝ yard for directional print)

- Binding: ¼ yard *or* 2 strips 2¼″ × width of fabric

- Batting: 13″ × 19″ Pellon 987F Fusible Fleece

The place mats feature fabrics from the Glimma collection by Lotta Jansdottr for Windham Fabrics and Quilter's Linen by Robert Kaufman Fabrics.

Print the Patterns

For the patterns, refer to the pullout. To adjust the printing, if necessary, refer to Reducing and Enlarging Patterns (page 13).

For each place mat, print the following patterns at 108% (the uppercase **E** is 4″ tall):

- Uppercase: **E, A, T**

Make the Letters

For sewing techniques, refer to How to Paper Piece (page 10).

1. Cut 1 strip × width of fabric for each strip size to start. Cut more as needed.

- Letters: 2″
- Background: 2″

2. Paper piece the letters.

3. Press, trim, and remove the paper.

Detail of *EAT* place mat

Put It Together

1. From background fabric:
   - Cut 2 strips 1½″ × width of fabric.
     Subcut 3 rectangles 1½″ × 11″ (B).
     Subcut 2 rectangles 1½″ × 19″ (C).
     Subcut 2 rectangles 1½″ × 4½″,
       and then trim to ⅞″ × 4½″ (A).

2. From center fabric:
   - Cut 1 rectangle 11″ × 12″, paying attention to the direction of the print (D).
   - Cut 1 rectangle 13″ × 19″ for the back of the place mat.

3. Sew A strips between the letters **E**, **A**, and **T**.

4. Sew B strips above and below **EAT**.

5. Sew piece D to the bottom of the **EAT** unit.

6. Sew a B strip to the bottom of piece D.

7. Sew a C strip to each side of the unit to complete the place mat top.

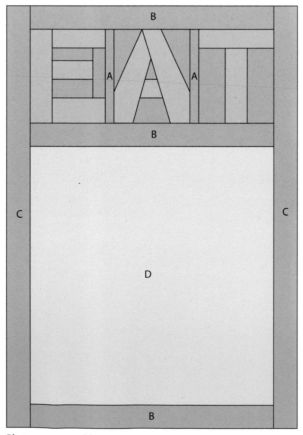

Place mat assembly

EAT place mats, 13˝ × 19˝ each

Ahh, the luxury of a cozy nap in the afternoon. Put your toes under this bed runner to keep them warm. Or turn it over for a different kind of heat!

Afternoon Snooze /
Afternoon Delight!

Finished reversible bed runner: 17½" × 70½"

Designed, pieced, and quilted by Sam Hunter, 2013

❋ GO SHOPPING!

- **Snooze background:**
  1⅛ yards taupe

- **Snooze words and
  border:** ¼ yard each of
  6 or more muted prints

- **Delight background:**
  1⅛ yards white

- **Delight words and
  border:** ¼ yard each of
  6 or more bright prints

- **Binding:** ½ yard print that
  goes with both sides

- **Optional backing:**
  1½ yards (if you choose
  to make a one-sided
  bed runner)

- **Batting:** 26" × 79"

The *Afternoon Snooze* quilt features fabrics from the World Tour collection
by Parson Gray for Westminster Fabrics. *Afternoon Delight!*, on the other
side, features fabrics from the Florence collection by Denyse Schmidt for
Westminster Fabrics.

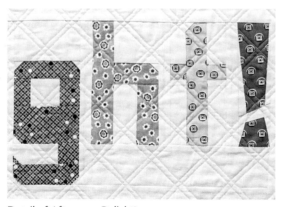

Detail of *Afternoon Delight!*

Print the Patterns

*For the patterns, refer to the pullout. To adjust
the printing, if necessary, refer to Reducing and
Enlarging Patterns (page 13).*

Print the following patterns at 180%
(the lowercase **a** is 4½" tall):

- Lowercase: **a** (2), **d**, **e** (4), **f** (2), **g**, **h**, **i**, **l**, **n** (5),
  o (6), **r** (2), **s**, **t** (3), **z**
- Punctuation: **!** (exclamation point)

Make the Letters

For sewing techniques, refer to How to Paper Piece (page 10).

1. Separate the letter patterns into two groups: **afternoon snooze** and **afternoon delight!**. Group the letters with the corresponding muted and bright fabrics.

2. Cut 1 strip × width of fabric from each letter fabric. For the background fabric, cut 1 strip × width of fabric for each strip size to start. Cut more as needed.
   - Letters: 2½˝ from each letter fabric
   - Background: 2˝, 2½˝, 3˝

3. Paper piece the letters.

4. Press, trim, and remove the paper.

Make the Words

afternoon snooze

1. From background fabric:
   - Cut 2 strips 1⅛˝ × width of fabric.
     Subcut 12 strips 1⅛˝ × 5˝ (A).
     Subcut 1 strip 1⅛˝ × 7¼˝ (B).

   - Cut 1 strip 2¾˝ × width of fabric.
     Subcut 1 rectangle 2¾˝ × 4¾˝ (C).
     Subcut 1 strip 2¾˝ × 25⅞˝ (D).

   - Cut 3 strips 3¾˝ × width of fabric.
     Subcut 2 strips 3¾˝ × 25¼˝ (E).
     Subcut 1 strip 3¾˝ × 36⅝˝ (F).
     Subcut 1 rectangle 3¾˝ × 11½˝ (G).

   - Cut 1 strip 1½˝ × width of fabric.
     Subcut 1 strip 1½˝ × 36⅝˝ (H).

   - Cut 1 strip 3½˝ × width of fabric.
     Subcut 2 rectangles 3½˝ × 11½˝ (J).

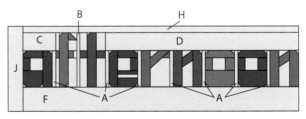

Join to afternoon.

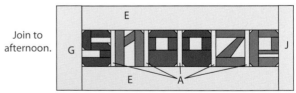

Detail of *Afternoon Snooze*

Detail of *Afternoon Snooze*

2. Sew an A strip to the right side of **a**.

3. Sew piece C to the top of **a**.

4. Sew strip B between **f** and **t**.

5. Sew **a** to **ft**.

6. Sew A strips to the left side of **e** and between **e**, **r**, **n**, **o**, **o**, and **n**.

7. Sew strip D to the top of **ernoon**.

8. Sew **aft** to **ernoon**.

9. Sew strip H to the top of **afternoon**.

10. Sew strip F to the bottom of **afternoon**.

11. Sew A strips between **s**, **n**, **o**, **o**, **z**, and **e**.

12. Sew E strips to the top and bottom of **snooze**.

13. Sew piece G between **afternoon** and **snooze**.

14. Sew a J piece to each end of **afternoon snooze**.

afternoon delight!

1. From background fabric:

- Cut 3 strips 1⅛″ × width of fabric.
  Subcut 7 strips 1⅛″ × 5″ (K).
  Subcut 8 strips 1⅛″ × 7¼″ (L).

- Cut 2 strips 2¾″ × width of fabric.
  Subcut 1 rectangle 2¾″ × 4¾″ (M).
  Subcut 2 rectangles 2¾″ × 4⅛″ (N)
  Subcut 1 strip 2¾″ × 25⅞″ (P).
  Subcut 1 rectangle 2¾″ × 12½″ (Q).
  Subcut 1 rectangle 2¾″ × 11″ (R).

- Cut 1 strip 3″ × width of fabric.
  Subcut 2 rectangles 3″ × 11½″ (S).

- Cut 2 strips 3¾″ × width of fabric.
  Subcut 1 strip 3¾″ × 36⅝″ (T).
  Subcut 1 rectangle 3¾″ × 11½″ (U).

- Cut 3 strips 1½″ × width of fabric.
  Subcut 1 strip 1½″ × 36⅝″ (V).
  Subcut 2 strips 1½″ × 26½″ (W).

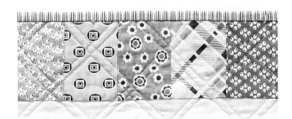

Detail of *Afternoon Delight!*

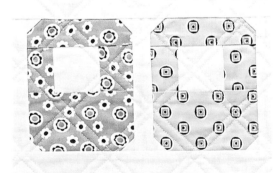

Detail of *Afternoon Delight!*

2. Sew a K strip to the right side of **a**.

3. Sew piece M to the top of **a**.

4. Sew an L strip between **f** and **t**.

5. Sew **a** to **ft**.

6. Sew K strips to the left side of **e** and between **e**, **r**, **n**, **o**, **o**, and **n**.

7. Sew strip P to the top of **ernoon**.

8. Sew **aft** to **ernoon**.

9. Sew strip V to the top of **afternoon**.

10. Sew strip T to the bottom of **afternoon**.

11. Sew N pieces to the top of **e** and **g**.

12. Sew L strips between **d**, **e**, **l**, and **i** and to the right side of **i**.

13. Sew piece Q to the bottom of **deli**.

14. Sew L strips to the left side of **h** and between **h**, **t**, and **!**.

15. Sew piece R to the bottom of **ht!**. Trim piece R as needed.

16. Sew **deli** to **g**.

17. Sew **delig** to **ht!**.

18. Sew W strips to the top and bottom of **delight!**.

19. Sew piece U between **afternoon** and **delight!**.

20. Sew an S strip to each end of **afternoon delight!**.

21. Measure and trim the word block to be 70½˝ long.

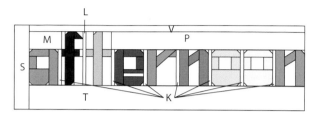

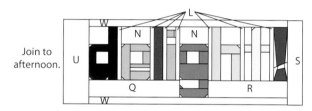

Join to afternoon.

Make the Borders

1. From the letter prints for **afternoon snooze**, cut the following for *one* side of the quilt:

■ Cut a minimum of 7 assorted strips 2½˝ × width of fabric.
    Subcut 70 rectangles 2½˝ × 3½˝.

2. Mixing up the fabrics, sew together 35 rectangles along the long sides to make the top border.

3. Repeat Step 2 to make the bottom border.

4. Sew the borders to the top and bottom of the word block.

5. Repeat Steps 1–4 for the **afternoon delight** side of the quilt.

Afternoon Snooze, 17½˝ × 70½˝

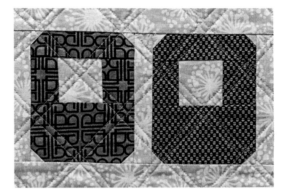

Detail of *Afternoon Snooze*

Afternoon Delight! (alternate side of *Afternoon Snooze*)

Detail of *Afternoon Delight!*

You can never have too many places to stash stuff, especially in the sewing studio. Make one of these buckets for yourself. Make them as gifts. Make them sassy. Make them personal. Fill them with stuff. Make more....

Oh Scrap!

Finished bucket: 9″ tall × 9½″ diameter   Designed, pieced, and quilted by Sam Hunter, 2013

✳ GO SHOPPING!

- **Outer bucket:**
  ⅝ yard light print

- **Bucket lining:**
  ⅜ yard coordinating print

- **Letter background:**
  ⅓ yard light (or dark)

- **Letters:** ¼ yard or scraps

- **Optional contrasting band as in STUFF** (page 122): 1″ × 24″ strip

- **Fusible fleece:**
  ⅔ yard 45″-wide Pellon 987F (white) or 987FB (black) Fusible Fleece

- **Timtex heavyweight interfacing:** 1 sheet 15″ × 18″ (or 9″ × 30″ from a bolt)

- **Muslin for joining Timtex:**
  7″ × 12″ rectangle of muslin or other fabric that will not show through the bucket fabrics

- **Fusible web:**
  7″ × 12″ rectangle of Steam-A-Seam 2

The *Oh Scrap!* bucket features fabrics from the Just My Type collection by Patty Young for Michael Miller Fabrics and Kona Cotton Solids by Robert Kaufman Fabrics.

The *Full of Knit* bucket features fabrics from the Collage collection by Carrie Bloomston of SUCH Designs for Windham Fabrics.

The *Stuff* bucket features fabrics from the Cameras and Dots collections by Michael Miller Fabrics and Kona Cotton Solids by Robert Kaufman Fabrics.

Print the Patterns

For the patterns, refer to the pullout. To adjust the printing, if necessary, refer to Reducing and Enlarging Patterns (page 13).

oh scrap!

1. Print **oh** in lowercase at 55% (the lowercase **o** is 1⅜″ tall).

2. Print **scrap** in lowercase and **!** at 75% (the lowercase **c** is 1⅞″ tall).

full of knit

1. Print **full of** in lowercase at 55% (the lowercase **u** is 1⅜″ tall).

2. Print **knit** in lowercase at 70% (the lowercase **n** is 1¾″ tall).

STUFF

Print **STUFF** in uppercase at 60% (the uppercase **U** is 2¼″ tall).

When designing a personalized word or phrase, give the letters a couple of inches of breathing room.

The word block for the bucket is 5½″ × 11″ finished, so design your words to be no larger than 4½″ × 10″.

To design and print your words at the correct size, refer to Designing Custom Text (page 30) and Reducing and Enlarging Patterns (page 13).

You can also add elements like stripes to the word block.

Make the Letters

For sewing techniques, refer to How to Paper Piece (page 10).

1. Cut 1 strip × width of fabric for each strip size to start. Cut more as needed.
   - Letters: 1½″
   - Background: 1½″, 2″

2. Paper piece the letters.

3. Press, trim, and remove the paper.

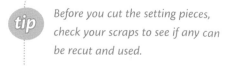

tip *Before you cut the setting pieces, check your scraps to see if any can be recut and used.*

Make the Words

oh scrap!

1. From letter background fabric:
   - Cut 2 strips ¾″ × width of fabric.
     Subcut 4 rectangles ¾″ × 2⅜″ (A).
     Subcut 1 rectangle ¾″ × 5⅝″ (H).
     Subcut 1 rectangle ¾″ × 9″ (J).
     Subcut 2 rectangles ¾″ × 11½″ (L).
     Subcut 1 rectangle ¾″ × 2½″ (M).

   - Cut 1 strip 2½″ × width of fabric.
     Subcut and trim 1 rectangle
       1⅝″ × 1⅛″ (B).
     Subcut 1 rectangle 2½″ × 4¼″ (C).
     Subcut 1 rectangle 2½″ × 3⅜″ (D).
     Subcut and trim 1 rectangle
       1¼″ × 1¾″ (E).
     Subcut and trim 1 rectangle
       1¼″ × 1½″ (F).
     Subcut and trim 1 rectangle
       1½″ × 7½″ (G).
     Subcut and trim 2 rectangles
       1¼″ × 5⅝″ (K).

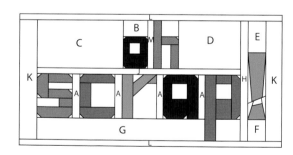

2. Sew piece B to the top of **o**.
   Trim as needed.

3. Sew piece M between **o** and **h**.

4. Sew piece C to the left side of **oh**.

5. Sew piece D to the right side of **oh**.

6. Sew A strips between **s**, **c**, **r**, and **a**.

7. Sew an A strip to the right side of **scra**.

8. Sew piece G to the bottom of **scra**.

9. Sew **p** to the right side of **scra**.

10. Sew strip J between **oh** and **scrap**. Trim as needed.

11. Sew piece E to the top of **!** and sew piece F to the bottom.

12. Sew strip H between **oh scrap** and **!**.

13. Sew a K strip to each side of **oh scrap!**. Trim to measure 11½˝ long.

14. Sew L strips to the top and bottom of **oh scrap!**.

full of knit

1. From letter background fabric:
   - Cut 1 strip ¾˝ × width of fabric.
     Subcut 3 rectangles ¾˝ × 11½˝ (A).

   - Cut 1 strip 3⅛˝ × width of fabric.
     Subcut 2 rectangles 3⅛˝ × 3½˝ (B).
     Subcut 3 rectangles 3⅛˝ × ¾˝ (C).
     Subcut and trim 2 rectangles
        2⅝˝ × 2¾˝ (D).
     Subcut and trim 4 rectangles
        2⅝˝ × ¾˝ (E).
     Subcut and trim 1 rectangle
        2⅝˝ × 1½˝ (F).
     Subcut and trim 2 rectangles
        1⅝˝ × 1¼˝ (G).
     Subcut and trim 1 rectangle
        2˝ × 1⅜˝ (H).

2. Sew a G piece to the top of **u** and **o**.

3. Sew E strips between **f**, **u**, **l**, and **l**.

4. Sew an E strip between **o** and **f**.

5. Sew piece F between **full** and **of**.

6. Sew a D piece to each side of **full of**.

7. Sew piece H to the top of **n**.

8. Sew C strips between **k**, **n**, **i**, and **t**.

9. Sew a B piece to each side of **knit**. Trim as needed.

10. Sew an A strip between **full of** and **knit**. Trim to 11½˝ wide.

11. Sew A strips to the top of **full of** and the bottom of **knit**.

STUFF

1. From letter background fabric:
   - Cut 1 strip 1¾″ × width of fabric.
     Subcut 2 rectangles 1¾″ × 11½″ (A).
     Subcut and trim 4 rectangles
     2¾″ × ¾″ (B).
     Subcut and trim 2 rectangles
     2¾″ × 1″ (C).

2. From contrast fabric:
   - Cut 2 rectangles ⅞″ × 11½″ (D).

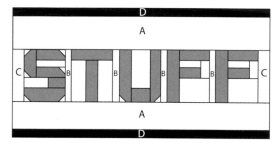

3. Sew B strips between **S**, **T**, **U**, **F**, and **F**.

4. Sew a C piece to each side of **STUFF**.

5. Sew A strips to the top and bottom
   of **STUFF**.

6. Sew D strips to the top and bottom
   of **STUFF**.

Put It Together

1. From outer bucket fabric:
   - Cut 1 strip 11¼″ × width of fabric.
     Subcut 2 rectangles 11¼″ × 10″ (A).
     Subcut 1 rectangle 11¼″ × 11½″;
     subcut to 11½″ × 1¾″ (B) and
     11½″ × 4½″ (C). (This will maintain
     the direction of the print when
     assembled.)

   - Cut a 10″ circle, using the quarter-circle
     pattern (page 126) to make a template.

2. From bucket lining fabric:
   - Cut 1 strip 11″ × width of fabric.
     Subcut 1 rectangle 11″ × 30⅜″.
     Subcut a 9½″ circle from the remainder
     of the strip, using the quarter-circle
     pattern (page 126) to make a template.

3. From fusible fleece:
   - Cut a strip 10″ × width of fleece.
     Subcut 1 rectangle 9″ × 29¾″.
     Subcut a 9½″ circle from the remainder
     of the strip, using the template made
     for the lining.

   - Cut a strip 9″ × width of fleece.
     Subcut 1 rectangle 9″ × 29¾″.
     Subcut a 9″ circle from the remainder
     of the strip, using the quarter-circle
     pattern (page 126) to make a template.

4. From the Timtex:
   - Cut 2 rectangles 9″ × 15″.
     Subcut a 1″ × 9″ strip from the
     end of 1 rectangle. Subcut into
     4 rectangles 1″ × 2¼″.

5. From muslin:
- Iron the fusible web onto one side of the muslin following the manufacturer's instructions.
- Cut 4 strips 1½″ × 11″.

6. Fuse the 9″ fleece circle to the wrong side of the 9½″ lining fabric circle, leaving ¼″ all around. This is the bottom of the bucket lining.

7. Fuse the 9½″ fleece circle to the wrong side of the 10″ outer fabric circle, leaving ¼″ all around. This is the bottom of the outer bucket.

MAKE THE OUTER BUCKET

1. Sew piece B to the bottom of the word block.

2. Sew piece C to the top of the word block.

3. Sew an A piece to each side of the word block.

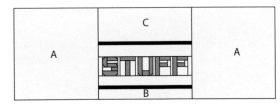

4. Along the top of the outer bucket, press ¼″ to the wrong side.

5. Following the manufacturer's instructions, fuse a 9″ × 29¾″ rectangle of fusible fleece to the wrong side of the outer bucket, placing it ¼″ from the bottom and both sides.

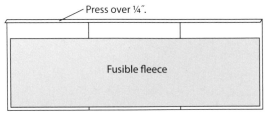

Press over ¼″.

Fusible fleece

6. Sew the 2 short ends of the outer bucket together to form a cylinder. Take care to keep the fusible fleece out of the seam.

7. Place 4 pins in the bottom edge of the outer bucket at "north, south, east, and west." Find these points by folding the cylinder flat and marking the edges, then folding the 2 marked edges together. You can use the seam as one of the compass points.

8. Place 4 pins in the outer bucket bottom at "north, south, east, and west."

9. With right sides together, fit the bottom circle into the bottom of the cylinder, matching the pins. Pin generously between the original 4 pins, easing the circle into place.

10. Sew the circle to the cylinder, making sure to sew the full ¼″ seam allowance without catching the fusible fleece in the seam.

11. Turn right side out and press.

MAKE THE BUCKET LINING

If your fabric has a directional print, note the direction. It must be upside down within the bucket for the cuff on the bucket to appear right side up.

1. From each bottom corner of the bucket lining fabric, measure 9½″ up the side edge and mark.

2. From each bottom corner, measure ½″ along the bottom edge and mark. Draw a line connecting the marks on each side. Cut on the line to remove a wedge from each corner.

3. From each bottom corner of the remaining fleece rectangle, measure ½″ along the bottom edge and mark. Draw a line connecting the marks on each side with the upper corners. Cut on the line to remove a wedge from each corner.

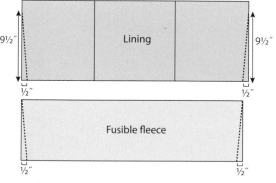

Wedge cutting diagram

4. Along the top of the bucket lining, press ¼″ to the wrong side.

5. Following the manufacturer's instructions, fuse the fleece to the wrong side of the bucket lining, placing it ¼″ from the bottom and sides.

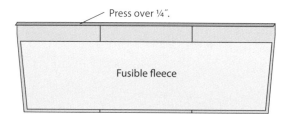

Press over ¼″.

Fusible fleece

6. Sew the short ends of the bucket lining together. Take care to keep the fusible fleece out of the seam.

7. Repeat Make the Outer Bucket, Steps 7–10 (page 123), to assemble the bucket lining. When you are finished, do not turn the lining right side out.

Roxane, 9″ tall × 9½″ diameter

MAKE THE INNER CYLINDER

1. Join the 2 Timtex rectangles along the 9″ sides using the fused muslin strips. Center a strip of the muslin/fusible web along the seam, fuse it, turn the ends over to the other side, and fuse the ends down across the back of the seam. Repeat from the other side of the seam with a second piece of muslin/fusible web and bring the ends back to the front. Allow to cool.

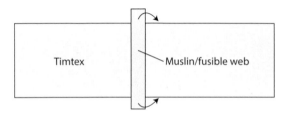

Timtex   Muslin/fusible web

2. Repeat Step 1 to join the remaining sides, forming a cylinder.

3. Sew a 1″ × 2¼″ piece of Timtex across the top and bottom of each joined seam. You can choose to work on either the inside or outside of the cylinder, whichever is easiest for you to manage. These small pieces help maintain the round shape of the cylinder and prevent it from visibly creasing at the joints.

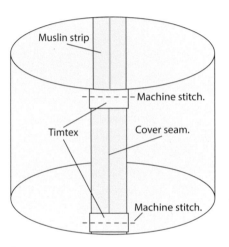

Muslin strip

Machine stitch.

Timtex   Cover seam.

Machine stitch.

ASSEMBLE THE BUCKET

1. Insert the Timtex cylinder into the outer bucket. Push the Timtex all the way to the bottom and smooth out the bucket sides.

2. Insert the bucket lining into the Timtex cylinder, matching the lining seam with the outer bucket seam, with wrong sides together.

3. Generously pin the tops of the outer bucket and lining together, tucking in the pressed-over ¼″ edges.

4. Topstitch ⅛″ from the top edge of the bucket.

5. Turn the cuff of the bucket to the outside. The fold should be even with the top of the Timtex. Smooth out the inside of the bucket.

6. Fill it with things!

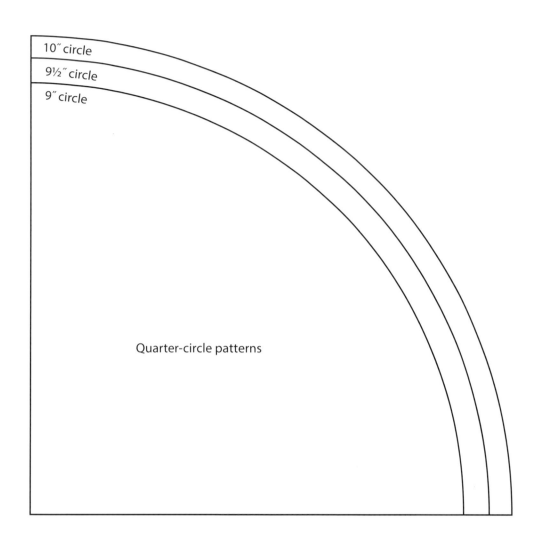

10″ circle

9½″ circle

9″ circle

Quarter-circle patterns

Oh Scrap!, 9˝ tall × 9½˝ diameter

Full of Knit, 9˝ tall × 9½˝ diameter

STUFF, 9˝ tall × 9½˝ diameter

Make it so. Make it happen. Sit right down at that machine and get started … make it sew! Captain Picard would approve.

Make It Sew!

Finished machine cover: 32½" × 16" (standard) or 32½" × 18" (oversized) Designed, pieced, and quilted by Sam Hunter, 2013

✳ GO SHOPPING!

- **Letter background:** ½ yard white

- **Letters and ties:** ¼ yard or 1 fat quarter each of 4 colors

- **Cover body:** ⅝ yard teal print (¾ yard for extra-large cover)

- **Backing:** ½ yard (⅝ yard for extra-large cover)

- **Pellon 987F (white) or 987FB (black) Fusible Fleece:** ½ yard (⅝ yard for extra-large cover)

This machine cover features fabrics from the Pin Spin collection by Michael Miller Fabrics and Kona Cotton Solids and Quilter's Linen by Robert Kaufman Fabrics.

Print the Patterns

For the patterns, refer to the pullout. To adjust the printing, if necessary, refer to Reducing and Enlarging Patterns (page 13).

1. Print the following patterns at 70% (the lowercase **a** is 1¾" tall):
   - Lowercase: **m**, **a**, **k**, **e**, **i**, **t**

2. Print the following patterns at 130% (the lowercase **s** is 3¼" tall):
   - Lowercase: **s**, **e**, **w**

3. Print **!** at 186% (7" tall).

Make the Letters

For sewing techniques, refer to How to Paper Piece (page 10).

1. Cut 1 strip × width of fabric for each strip size to start. Cut more as needed.
   - Letters: 1¾"
   - Background: 1½", 2¼"
   - Exclamation point: 3"

2. Paper piece the letters.

3. Press, trim, and remove the paper.

 *Skip pattern piece 2 on the **i**; it's just too tiny!*

make it yours

When designing a personalized word or phrase, give the letters a couple of inches of breathing room.

The word block of the machine cover is 8½" × 14" finished, so design your words to be no larger than 7" × 12".

To design and print your words at the correct size, refer to Designing Custom Text (page 30) and Reducing and Enlarging Patterns (page 13).

Make the Words

SET THE LETTERS

1. From letter background fabric:

- Cut 1 strip ⅞" × width of fabric.
  Subcut 3 rectangles ⅞" × 2¼" (A).
  Subcut and trim 1 rectangle
  ¾" × 3⅛" (B).

- Cut 1 strip 1⅝" × width of fabric.
  Subcut 1 rectangle 1⅝" × 10¾" (C).
  Subcut and trim 1 rectangle
  1⅜" × 4⅝" (D).
  Subcut and trim 1 rectangle
  1⅜" × 2¼" (E).
  Subcut and trim 1 rectangle
  1½" × 3⅛" (F).
  Subcut and trim 2 rectangles
  1⅛" × 3¾" (G).
  Subcut and trim 1 rectangle
  1" × 7½" (H).

- Cut 2 strips 1¼" × width of fabric.
  Subcut 2 rectangles 1¼" × 13⅛" (J).
  Subcut 2 rectangles 1¼" × 9" (K).

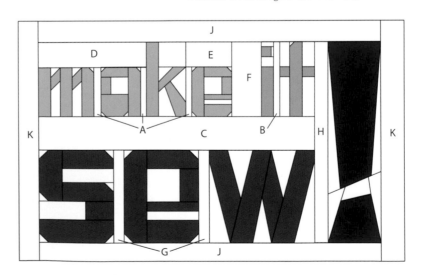

2. Sew A pieces to the right side of **m** and the right side of **a**.

3. Sew **m** to **a**.

4. Sew piece D to the top of **ma**.

5. Sew **ma** to **k**.

6. Sew an A piece to the left side of **e**.

7. Sew piece E to the top of **e**.

8. Sew **mak** to **e**.

9. Sew piece B between **i** and **t**.

10. Sew piece F between **make** and **it**. The word unit should measure 10¾″ long.

11. Sew G pieces between **s**, **e**, and **w**.

12. Sew piece C between **make it** and **sew**.

13. Sew piece H to the right side of **make it sew**.

14. Sew the exclamation point to the right side of **make it sew**.

15. Sew J pieces to the top and bottom of **make it sew!**.

16. Sew a K piece to each side of **make it sew!**. The unit should measure 14½″ × 9″. Trim if necessary.

Put It Together
MAKE THE COVER BODY

The dimensions for the oversized machine are in parentheses.

1. From cover body fabric:
   - Cut 1 strip 1½″ (2½″) × width of fabric. Subcut 2 strips 1½″ (2½″) × 9″ (A).
   - Cut 1 strip 16½″ (18½″) × width of fabric. Subcut 1 rectangle 16½″ (18½″) × 22½″ (B). Subcut 1 strip 16½″ (18½″) × 2½″ (C).

2. From fusible fleece:
   - Cut 1 strip 16″ (18″) × width of fabric. Subcut 1 rectangle 16″ (18″) × 32½″.

3. From backing fabric:
   - Cut 1 strip 16½″ (18½″) × width of fabric. Subcut 1 rectangle 16½″ (18½″) × 33″. Set aside until time to assemble the cover.

4. Sew an A strip to each side of the word block (see the front cover assembly diagram, page 132).

5. Sew piece B to the top of the word block.

6. Sew strip C to the bottom of the word block to complete the front cover.

7. Iron the fusible fleece to the wrong side of the front cover, centering it to leave a ¼″ seam allowance on all edges.

MAKE THE TIES

1. From each of the 4 letter fabrics, cut 1 rectangle 2˝ × 12½˝.

2. On each rectangle, press under ¼˝ at a short end.

3. Press the pieces in half along the length with wrong sides together.

4. Open each piece and fold the raw edges in to meet the middle crease; press again.

5. Topstitch through the middle down the length of each tie.

tip   *You can use ribbon or twill tape to make your ties if you prefer.*

ASSEMBLE THE COVER

1. Pin the ties to the front cover approximately 7˝ from the raw edge on both sides. The front ties should align with the space between **make it** and **sew** in the word block.

2. Align the raw edge of each tie to the raw edge of the cover and baste in place with a scant ¼˝ seam allowance.

3. With right sides together, pin the backing fabric to the front cover. Sew together using a ¼˝ seam allowance, leaving a 6˝ opening at the end opposite the word block. Be careful not to catch the loose ends of the ties in this seam.

4. Turn right side out through the 6˝ opening and press well.

5. Topstitch ⅛˝ from the outer edge all the way around the cover.

6. Quilt as desired, or skip the quilting if you prefer.

Front cover assembly

Make It Sew!, 32½″ × 16″

APPENDIX

Making a Sleeve

Make and add a hanging sleeve before binding your quilt.

1. Measure the entire width of the quilt along the edge where the sleeve will go. Call this number S and subtract 1″ to get the length to cut.

   L (length of sleeve fabric) = S – 1″

2. Measure the width of the slat or dowel that you plan to use inside the sleeve. Call this number D and multiply by 2; then add 1½″ to get the width to cut.

   W (width of the sleeve fabric) = (2 × D) + 1½″

3. Cut sleeve fabric L × W.

4. Fold over a scant ¼″ twice on the short ends, press, and topstitch to hem each end.

5. With wrong sides together, press in half along the longest dimension.

6. Pin to the top back of the quilt, with the raw edges aligned with the edge of the quilt.

7. Place the rod in the sleeve to check the fit. If the sleeve feels too loose, trim the long raw edges and refit. The rod should slide easily and not be so tight that it distorts the front of the quilt.

8. Sew the sleeve to the quilt, using a scant ¼″ seam so that it will fit inside the binding seam.

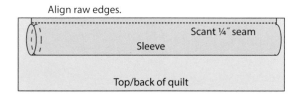

Align raw edges.

Scant ¼″ seam

Sleeve

Top/back of quilt

9. After the binding is attached, sew the lower edge of the sleeve to the quilt back by hand, using a blind stitch.

Snowball Corners

This is an easy way to add a triangle to a corner without having to cut triangles!

1. Chalk a diagonal line on the wrong side of the square that will become the triangle.

2. With right sides together, place the marked square on the corner, matching the raw edges.

3. Sew along the chalked line and trim to a ¼″ seam allowance.

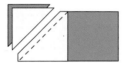

4. Press the triangle into place.

Diagonal Seams

Use this technique to make continuous strips for binding or long pieces in a quilt top.

1. With right sides together, place the end of one strip on top of another and sew diagonally. On larger strips, mark the line first before sewing.

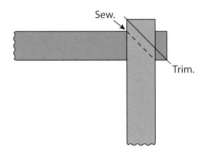

2. Trim to a ¼″ seam allowance and press the seams open.

3. For binding, press the entire strip in half lengthwise with wrong sides together.

Punctuation, Characters, and Symbols

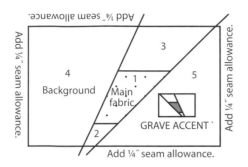

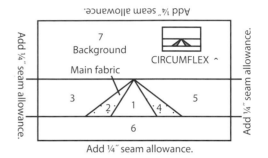

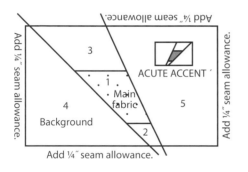

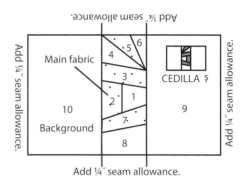

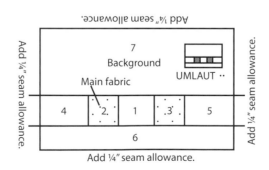

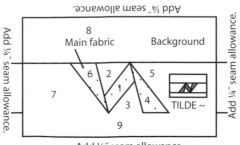

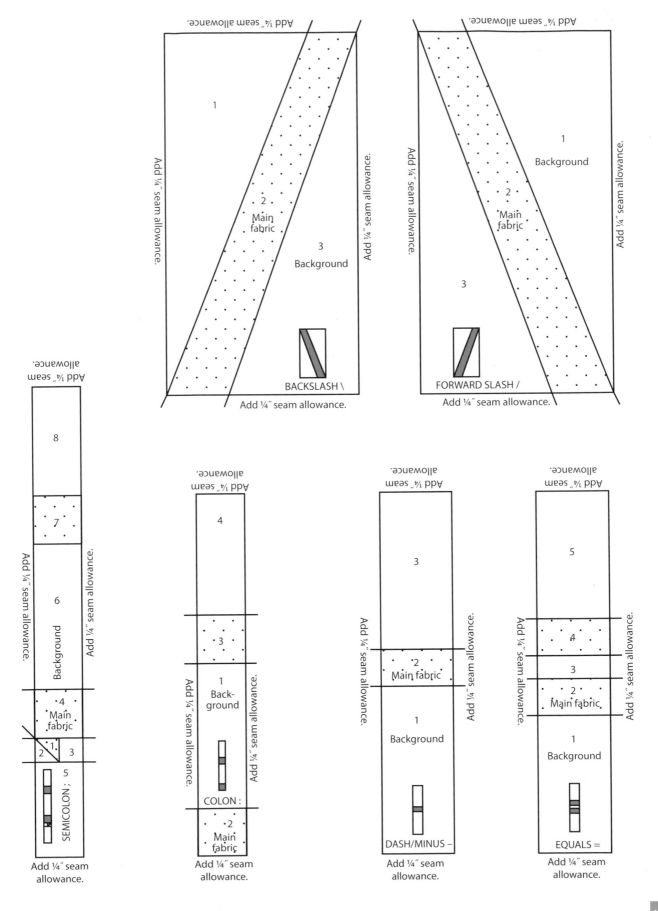

Add ¼" seam allowance.

Add ¼" seam allowance.

1

2
Main
fabric

3
Background

Add ¼" seam allowance.

Add ¼" seam allowance.

BACKSLASH \

1
Background

2
Main
fabric

3

Add ¼" seam allowance.

FORWARD SLASH /

Add ¼" seam allowance.

Add ¼" seam allowance.

8

7

6
Background

4
Main
fabric

2   1   3

5

SEMICOLON ;

Add ¼" seam
allowance.

Add ¼" seam allowance.

4

3

1
Back-
ground

2
Main
fabric

COLON :

Add ¼" seam
allowance.

Add ¼" seam allowance.

3

2
Main fabric

1
Background

DASH/MINUS –

Add ¼" seam
allowance.

Add ¼" seam allowance.

5

4

3

2
Main fabric

1
Background

EQUALS =

Add ¼" seam
allowance.

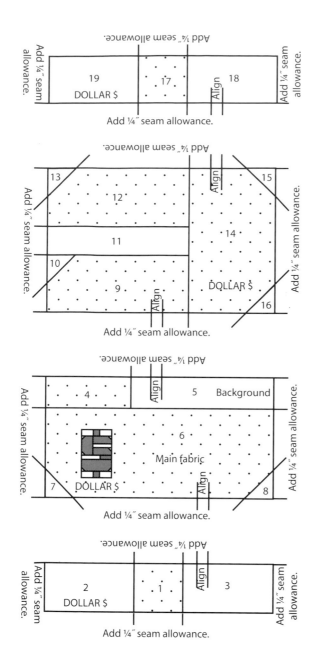

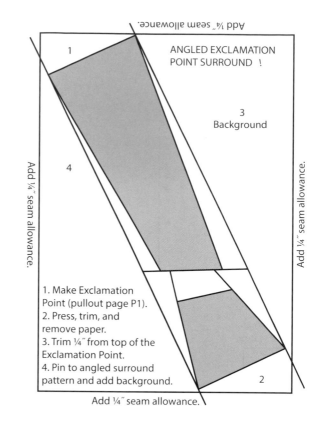

ANGLED EXCLAMATION
POINT SURROUND !

3
Background

4

1. Make Exclamation
Point (pullout page P1).
2. Press, trim, and
remove paper.
3. Trim ¼″ from top of the
Exclamation Point.
4. Pin to angled surround
pattern and add background.

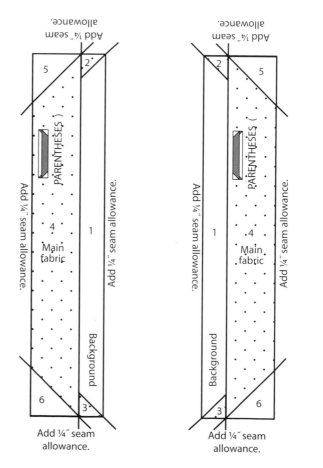

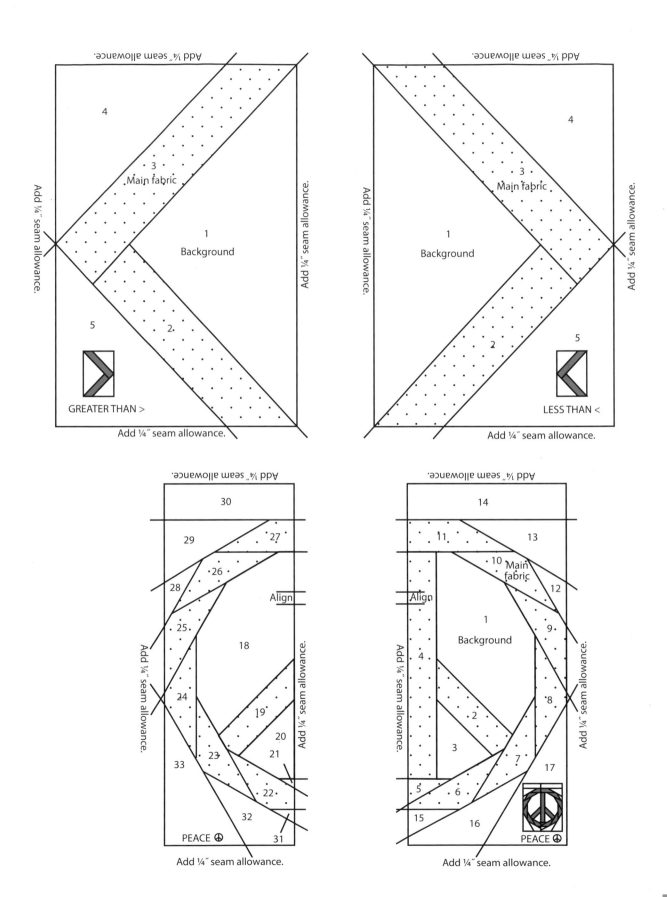

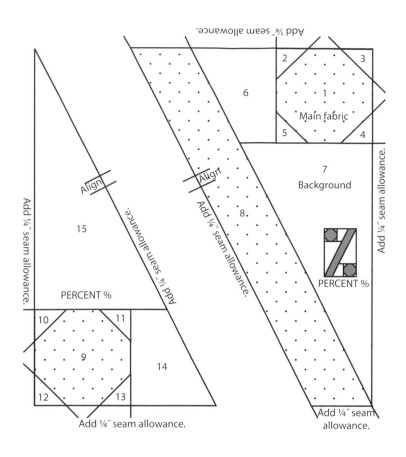

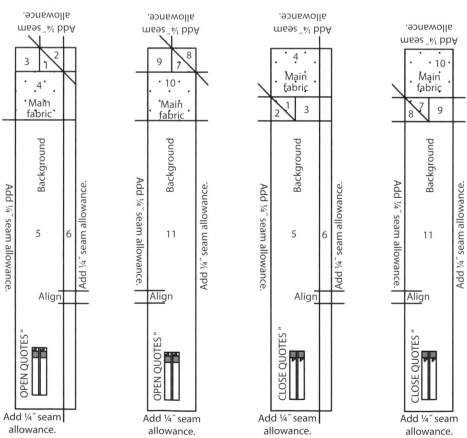

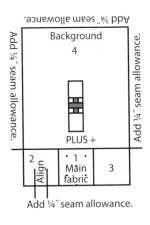

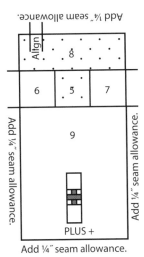

Add ¼" seam allowance.

Add ¼" seam allowance.

Add ¼" seam allowance.

Add ¼" seam allowance.

Add ¼" seam allowance.

RESOURCES

Thank you to the following companies for their generous help and great products.

FABRIC

Andover Fabrics
andoverfabrics.com

Art Gallery Fabrics
artgalleryquilts.com

Michael Miller Fabrics
michaelmillerfabrics.com

Moda Fabrics
unitednotions.com

P&B Textiles
pbtex.com

Robert Kaufman Fabrics
robertkaufman.com

Stof A/S Denmark
stof-dk.com

Westminster Fibers
westminsterfibers.com

Windham Fabrics
windhamfabrics.com

NOTIONS

C&T Publishing
ctpub.com
*Simple Foundations Translucent
Vellum Paper; Carol Doak's
Foundation Paper; Timtex*

Pellon
pellonprojects.com
*Pellon Fusible Fleece and
Sheerweight interfacing*

Warm Company
warmcompany.com
*Sam uses Warm & Natural
batting in all her projects.*

EQUIPMENT

Janome
janome.com
Janome Horizon 8900 QCP

Olfa
olfa.com
Olfa cutters and scissors

Oliso
oliso.com
Oliso 1600 TG iron

REFERENCE BOOKS

C&T Publishing
ctpub.com
  *First Steps to Free-Motion
  Quilting* by Christina Cameli
  (Stash Books)

  *Make Your First Quilt
  with M'Liss Rae Hawley*

  *Start Quilting
  with Alex Anderson*

DVDS

C&T Publishing
ctpub.com
  *Alex Anderson Teaches You
  to Start Quilting*

  *Diana McClun & Laura Nownes
  Teach You Beginning
  Quiltmaking*

Photo by Larry Lytle

ABOUT THE AUTHOR

Sam Hunter is a fiber artist and quilt designer who considers her sewing machine to be the ultimate power tool. Sam spent her formative years hopping back and forth between her native England and the United States. She settled on the West Coast in her twenties, after the birth of her son, Steve.

Sam started sewing when she was seven and hasn't really stopped since. She considers herself fortunate to have been taught the needlecrafts from a lineage of creative family members and womenfolk. She began quilting in 1989 and teaching shortly thereafter.

Sam earned her MFA in fiber arts in 2010 and is thrilled to have written her last-ever term paper. The fact that she gleefully escaped formal academia only to then write this book is a situation whose irony is not lost on her.

Sam launched Hunter's Design Studio, her pattern design company, in 2011 and is the Word Girl behind the Sew Sassy designs. She is a fun and humorous speaker and a relaxed and encouraging teacher. Sam is also the founder of We Are $ew Worth It, a movement to help quiltmakers and sewists earn a living wage for the things they make. You can reach her at huntersdesignstudio.com.

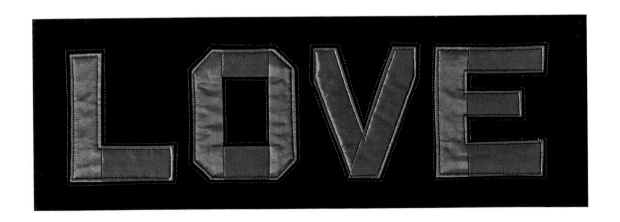

stash BOOKS ®

fabric arts for a handmade lifestyle

If you're craving beautiful authenticity in a time of mass-production...Stash Books is for you. Stash Books is a line of how-to books celebrating fabric arts for a handmade lifestyle. Backed by C&T Publishing's solid reputation for quality, Stash Books will inspire you with contemporary designs, clear and simple instructions, and engaging photography.

www.ctpub.com